The Swiss Family Perelman

by S. J. Perelman

DRAWINGS BY AL HIRSCHFELD

THE LYONS PRESS

Copyright © 2000 by The Lyons Press

Cover image and all interior illustrations © Al Hirschfeld, art reproduced by
special arrangement with Hirschfeld's exclusive representative,
The Margo Feiden Galleries Ltd., New York

ALL RIGHTS RESERVED.
No part of this book may be reproduced in any manner whatsoever without the
express written consent of the publisher, except in the case of brief excerpts in
critical reviews and articles. All inquiries should be addressed to: The Lyons Press,
123 West 18 Street, New York, NY 10011.

Printed in the United States of America

Originally published in 1950 by Simon & Schuster

10 9 8 7 6 5 4 3 2 1

The Library of Congress Cataloging-in-Publication Data is available on file.

To Ted Patrick

AVAILABLE FROM THE LYONS PRESS
BY S. J. PERELMAN:

Baby, It's Cold Inside

The Last Laugh

The Rising Gorge

The Swiss Family Perelman

Table of Contents

The Swiss Family Perelman

1

Rancors Aweigh

S EVEN HUNDRED TONS of icy green water curled
off the crest of the California ground swell and struck
with malignant fury at the starboard plates of the S. S.
President Cleveland, westbound out of San Francisco
for Honolulu, Manila, and Hong Kong. Midway along
its deserted promenade, huddled in a blanket, a soli-
tary passenger sprawled in his deck-chair, pondering
between spasmodic intakes of breath the tangled web
of circumstance that had enmeshed him. To even the
most cursory eye—and there was no shortage of cursory

*What grotesque tale
lurked behind that penetrable mask?*

eyes among the stewards hurrying past—it was instantly apparent that the man was exceptional, a *rara avis*. Under a brow purer than that of Michelangelo's David, capped by a handful of sparse and greasy hairs, brooded a pair of fiery orbs, glittering like zircons behind ten-cent-store spectacles. His superbly chiseled lips, ordinarily compressed in a grim line that bespoke indomitable will, at the moment hung open flaccidly, revealing row on row of pearly white teeth and a slim, patrician tongue. In the angle of the obdurate outthrust jaw, buckwheat-flecked from the morning meal, one read quenchless resolve, a nature scornful of compromise and dedicated to squeezing the last nickel out of any enterprise. The body of a Greek god, each powerful muscle the servant of his veriest whim, rippled beneath the blanket, stubbornly disputing every roll of the ship. And yet this man, who by sheer poise and magnetism had surmounted the handicap of almost ethereal beauty and whose name, whispered in any chancellery in Europe, was a talisman from Threadneedle Street to the Shanghai Bund, was prey to acute misery. What grotesque tale lurked behind that penetrable mask? What dark forces had moved to speed him on his desperate journey, what scarlet thread in Destiny's twisted skein?

It was a story of betrayal, of a woman's perfidy beside which the recidivism of Guy Fawkes, Major André, and the infamous Murrel paled to child's play. That the woman should have been my own wife was harrowing enough. More bitter than aloes, however,

3

was the knowledge that as I lay supine in my deck-chair, gasping out my life, the traitress herself sat complacently fifty feet below in the dining saloon, bolting the table d'hôte luncheon and lampooning me to my own children. Her brazen effrontery, her heartless rejection of one who for twenty years had worshiped her this side idolatry and consecrated himself to indulging her merest caprice, sent a shudder through my frame. Coarse peasant whom I had rescued from a Ukrainian wheat-field, equipped with shoes, and ennobled with my name, she had rewarded me with the Judas kiss. Reviewing for the hundredth time the horrid events leading up to my imbroglio, I scourged myself with her duplicity and groaned aloud.

The actual sell-out had taken place one autumn evening three months before in New York. Weary of pub-crawling and eager to recapture the zest of courtship, we had stayed home to leaf over our library of bills, many of them first editions. As always, it was chock-full of delicious surprises: overdrafts, modistes' and milliners statements my cosset had concealed from me, charge accounts unpaid since the Crusades. If I felt any vexation, however, I was far too cunning to admit it. Instead, I turned my pockets inside out to feign insolvency, smote my forehead distractedly in the tradition of the Yiddish theater, and quoted terse abstracts from the bankruptcy laws. But fiendish feminine intuition was not slow to divine my true feelings. Just as I had uncovered a bill from Hattie Carnegie for a brocaded bungalow apron and was brandishing it under her nose, my wife suddenly turned pettish.

"Sixteen dollars!" I was screaming. "Gold lamé you need yet! Who do you think you are, Catherine of Aragon? Why don't you rip up the foyer and pave it in malachite?" With a single dramatic gesture, I rent open my shirt. "Go ahead!" I shouted. "Milk me—drain me dry! Marshalsea prison! A pauper's grave!"

"Ease off before you perforate your ulcer," she enjoined. "You're waking up the children."

"You think sixteen dollars grows on trees?" I pleaded, seeking to arouse in her some elementary sense of shame. "*Corpo di Bacco,* for sixteen dollars a family like ours could live in Siam a whole year! With nine servants to boot!"

"And you're the boy who could boot 'em," my wife agreed. "Listen, ever since you and that other poolroom loafer Hirschfeld got back from your trip around the world last year, all I've heard is Siam, morning, noon, and night. Lover, let us not dissemble longer. *Je m'en fiche de Siam.*"

"Oh, is that so?" I roared. "Well, I wish I were back there this minute! Those gentle, courteous people, those age-old temples, those placid winding canals overhung with acacia——" Overhung with nostalgia and a little cordial I had taken to ward off a chill, I gave way to racking sobs. And then, when my defenses were down and I was at my most vulnerable, the woman threw off the veneer of civilization and struck like a puff adder.

"O.K.," she said briskly. "Let's go."

5

"Go ahead!" I shouted.
"Milk me—drain me dry!"

"Go?" I repeated stupidly. "Go where?"

"To Siam, of course," she returned. "Where'd you think I meant—Norumbega Park?" For a full fifteen seconds I stared at her, unable to encompass such treachery.

"Are you crazy?" I demanded, trembling. "How would I make a living there? What would we eat?"

"Those mangosteens and papayas you're always prating about," she replied. "If the breadfruit gives out, you're still spry enough to chop cotton."

"B-but the kiddies!" I whimpered, seeking to arouse her maternal sense. "What about their schooling— their clay and rhythms? Who'll teach them to blow glass and stain those repugnant tie-racks, all the basic techniques they need to grow up into decent, useful citizens?"

"I'll buy a book on it," she said carelessly.

"Yes, do," I urged, "and while you're at it, buy one on the snakes and lizards of Southeast Asia. Geckos under your pillow, cobras in the bathtub—not that there *are* any bathtubs—termites, ants, scorpions——"

"You'll cope with them," she asserted. "You did all right with that viper on Martha's Vineyard last summer. The one in the electric-blue swim-suit and the pancake make-up."

"I see no reason to drag personalities into this," I thundered. Deftly changing the subject, I explained as patiently as I could that Siam was a vast malarial marsh, oppressively hot and crowded with underprivileged folk scratching out a submarginal existence.

7

"You and I would stifle there, darling," I went on. "It's a cultural Sahara. No theaters, no art shows, no symphony concerts——"

"By the way," she observed irrelevantly (women can never absorb generalities), "how was that symphony you attended Tuesday at the Copa? You were seen with another music-lover, a lynx-eyed mannequin in black sequins featuring a Lillian Russell balcony."

"I brand that as a lie," I said quietly, turning my back to remove a baseball constricting my larynx. "A dastardly, barefaced lie."

"Possibly," she shrugged. "We'll know better when the Wideawake Agency develops the negative. In any case, Buster, your next mail address is Bangkok." In vain to instance the strife and rebellion sweeping Asia, the plagues and political upheaval; with the literal-mindedness of her sex, the stubborn creature kept casting up some overwrought declaration I had made to the effect that there was not a subway or a psychoanalyst north of Singapore.

"No," I said savagely, "nor a pediatrician, an orthodontist, or a can of puréed spinach in a thousand miles."

"That's what I've been dreaming of," she murmured. "Keep talking. The more you say, the lovelier it sounds." At last, spars shot away and my guns silenced, I prepared to dip my ensign, but not without one final rapier thrust.

"Well, you've made your bed," I said cruelly. "I wash my hands. Bye-bye Martinis." The blow told; I saw her blanch and lunged home. "There's not a

drop of French vermouth between San Francisco and
Saint Tropez." For an instant, as she strove with the
animal in her, my fate hung in the balance. Then,
squaring her shoulders, her magnificent eyes blazing
defiance, she flung the shaker into the grate, smashing
it to smithereens.

"Anything you can do, I can do better," she said
in a voice that rang like metal. "Fetch up the seven-
league boots. Thailand, here I come."

Had the ex-Vicereine of India attended the Durbar
in a G-string, it would have occasioned less tittle-tattle
than the casual revelation to our circle that we were
breaking camp to migrate to the Land of the White
Elephant. "She dassen't show her face at the Colony,"
the tongues clacked. "They say he smokes two catties
of yen shee gow before breakfast. *In Reno veritas.*"
Rumors flew thick and fast. They ranged from snig-
gered allusions to the bar sinister to reports that we
were actually bound for the leper colony at Molokai,
the majority opinion holding that we were lammisters
from the FBI. The more charitable among our friends
took it upon themselves to scotch these old wives'
tales. "He's merely had a nervous breakdown," they
said loyally. "You can tell by the way he drums his
fingers when she's talking." Our children, they added,
were not real albinos, nor was it true I had been made
contact man for a white slave ring in Saigon. I was
much too yellow.

The reaction of the bairns was equally heart-warming. When the flash came that they were shortly transplanting to the Orient, they received it impassively. Adam, a sturdy lad of twelve, retired to his den, barricaded the door with a bureau, and hid under the bed with Flents in his ears in readiness for head-hunters. His sister Abby, whose geography at ten was still fairly embryonic, remained tractable until she discovered that Siam was not an annex of Macy's. She thereupon spread-eagled herself on the parquet and howled like a muezzin, her face tinted a terrifying blue. Toward evening the keening subsided and both were cajoled into taking a little nourishment through a tube. On discussing the matter tranquilly, I was gratified to find they had been laboring under a misapprehension. They had supposed we were going to discontinue their arithmetic and spelling, a situation they regarded as worse than death. When I convinced them that, on the contrary, they might do five hours of homework daily even en route, their jubilation was unbounded. They promptly contrived wax effigies of their parents and, puncturing them with pins, intoned a rubric in which the phrase "hole in the head" recurred from time to time.

Ignoring the tradesmen who, under the curious delusion that we were about to shoot the moon, crowded in to collect their accounts, we fell to work assembling the gear necessary for an extended stay out East. Perhaps my most difficult task was to dissuade the memsahib from taking along her eighty-six-piece Royal Doulton dinner service. I tried to explain that we would probably crouch on our hams in the dust and gnaw

*They promptly contrived
wax effigies of their parents.*

dried fish wrapped in a pandanus leaf, but you can sooner tame the typhoon than sway the bourgeois mentality. Within a week, our flat was waist-high in potato graters, pressure cookers, pop-up toasters, and poultry shears; to the whine of saws and clang of hammers, crews of carpenters boxed everything in sight, including the toilet, for shipment overseas. My wife's cronies, lured by the excitement like bears to wild honey, clustered about loading her with dress patterns, recipes for chowchow, and commissions for Shantung and rubies, while children scrambled about underfoot flourishing marlinspikes and igniting shipwreck flares. Through the press circulated my insurance broker, who had taken the bit in his teeth and was excitedly underwriting everyone against barratry and heartburn. Doctors bearing Martinis in one hand and hypodermics in the other immunized people at will; a cauldron of noodles steamed in a corner and an enterprising Chinese barber worked apace shaving heads. The confusion was unnerving. You would have sworn some nomad tribe like the Torguts was on the move.

A lifelong gift of retaining my aplomb under stress, nevertheless, aided me to function smoothly and efficiently. Cucumber-cool and rocket-swift, canny as Sir Basil Zaharoff, I set about leasing our farm in the Delaware Valley and our New York apartment. The problem of securing responsible tenants was a thorny one, but I met it brilliantly. The farm, naturally, was the easier to dispose of, there being a perennial demand for dank stone houses, well screened by poison sumac, moldering on an outcropping of red shale. Various inducements were forthcoming; ultimately, by paying a friend six hundred dollars and threatening to expose his extramarital capers, I gained his grudging consent to visit it occasionally. Disposing of our scatter in town, though, was rather more complex. The renting agents I consulted were blunt. The rooms were too large and sunny, they warned me; sublessees were not minded to run the risk of snow blindness. Washington Square, moreover, was deficient in traffic noise and monoxide, and in any event, the housing shortage had evaporated twelve minutes before. Of course, they would try, but it was a pity our place wasn't a warehouse. Everybody wanted warehouses.

The first prospects to appear were two rigidly corseted and excessively genteel beldames in caracul who tiptoed through the stash as gingerly as though it were a Raines Law hotel. It developed that they were scouts for a celebrated Hungarian pianist named Larczny, and their annoyance on learning that we owned no concert grand was marked. I observed amiably that inasmuch as Larczny had begun his career playing for throw money at Madame Rosebud's on Bienville Street, he might feel at home with the beer rings on our Minipiano. The door had hardly slammed shut before it was reopened by a quartet of behemoths from Georgia Tech. Wiping the residue of pot-likker from his chin with his sleeve, their spokesman offered to engage the premises as a bachelor apartment. The deal bogged down when I refused to furnish iron spiders for their fatback and worm gears for their still.

Interest the next couple of days was sporadic. A furtive gentleman, who kept the collar of his Chesterfield turned up during the interview, was definitely beguiled, but did not feel our floor would sustain the weight of a flat-bed press. He evidently ran some sort of small engraving business, cigar-store coupons as I understood it. Our hopes rose when Sir Hamish Sphincter, chief of the British delegation to United Nations, cabled from the *Queen Elizabeth* earmarking the rooms for his stay. Unfortunately, on arriving to inspect our digs, the baronet and his lady found them in a somewhat disordered state. Our janitor, in a hailstorm of plaster, was just demolishing the bathroom wall to get at a plumbing stoppage. By the time he dredged up the multiplication tables the children had cached there, Sir Hamish was bowling toward the Waldorf. We never actually met the person who rented the flat after our departure, but his manners were described as exquisite and his faro bank, until the law knocked it over, was said to be unrivaled in downtown Manhattan. I still wear on my watch-chain a .38 slug which creased the mantelpiece and one of his patrons, though not in the order named.

Dusk was settling down on Washington Square that early January afternoon and a chill wind soughed through the leafless trees as I marshaled our brave little band for the take-off. Trench-coated and Burberryed,

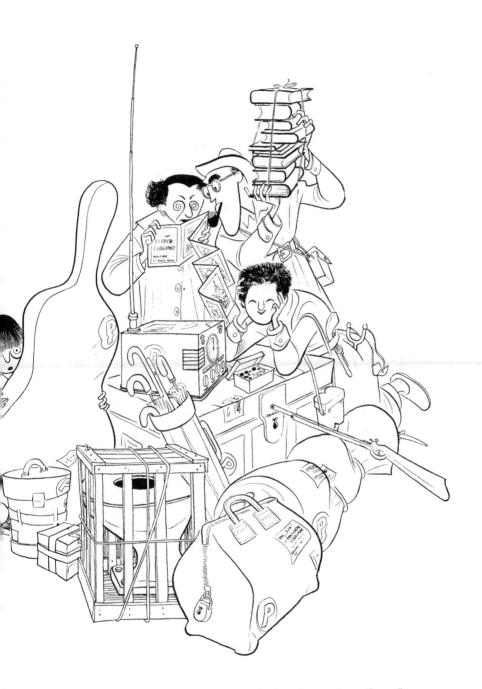

I marshaled our brave little band for the take-off.

festooned with binoculars, Rolleiflexes, sextants, hygrometers, and instruments for sounding the ocean floor, we were a formidable sight. The adults, their nerves honed to razor sharpness by weeks of barbital and bourbon, were as volatile as nitroglycerine; the slightest opposition flung them into apocalyptic rages followed by floods of tears. Without having covered a single parasang, the children had already accumulated more verdigris and grime than if they had traversed Cambodia on foot. The bandage on Adam's hand acquired in a last-minute chemistry experiment had unwound, but he was dexterously managing to engorge popcorn, read a comic, and maneuver an eelspear at the same time. Abby, bent double under her three-quarter-size 'cello, snuffled as her current beau, a hatchet-faced sneak of eleven, pledged eternal fealty. Heaped by the curb were fourteen pieces of baggage exclusive of trunks; in the background, like figures in an antique frieze, stood the janitor, the handyman, and the elevator operators, their palms mutely extended. I could see that they were too choked with emotion to speak, these men who I know not at what cost to themselves had labored to withhold steam from us and jam our dumbwaiters with refuse. Finally one grizzled veteran, bolder than his fellows, stepped forward with an obsequious tug at his forelock.

"We won't forget this day, sir," the honest chap said, twisting his cap in his gnarled hands. "Will we, mates?" A low growl of assent ran round the circle. "Many's the time we've carried you through that lobby and a reek of juniper off you a man could smell five miles down wind. We've seen some strange sights in this house and we've handled some spectacular creeps; it's a kind of a microcosm like, you might say. But we want you to know that never, not even in the nitrate fields of Chile, the smelters of Nevada, or the sweat-shops of the teeming East Side, has there been a man——" His voice broke and I stopped him gently.

"Friends," I said huskily, "I'm not rich in worldly goods, but let me say this—what little I have is mine. If you ever need anything, whether jewels, money, or negotiable securities, remember these words: you're barking up the wrong tree. Geronimo."

Their cheers were still ringing in my ears twenty minutes later as our cab swerved down the ramp into Pennsylvania Station. Against the hushed cacophony of the Map Room, I began to hear another and more exotic theme, the tinkle of gamelans and the mounting whine of the anopheles mosquito. The overture was ending. The first movement, *molto con citronella,* had begun.

"Friends, I'm not rich in worldly goods, but let me say this . . .
What little I have is mine."

2

Low Bridge—Everybody Down

T HE ENGINEER of the *Admiral,* crack flier of the Pennsylvania's New York-Chicago run, leaned out of the window of his cab, cast a practiced eye at the moonlit, rolling Indiana farmland speeding past, and withdrawing his head, addressed the conductor in a brogue that was an almost equal blend of John Jamieson and County Clare.

"Faix, and 'tis the exthraordinary request yiz is afther makin'," he observed, wiping his honest Hibernian countenance with a capacious red bandanna and abandoning his accent to make his dialogue less nerve-racking to the reader. "Am I to understand that you wish me to slow down abruptly so as to jolt the everlasting daylights out of the occupant of the upper berth in Room A, Car 138, a sorely tried paterfamilias tropic-bound as the result of a woman's relentless nagging, an aching desire to escape from the treadmill, and a callow romanticism pardonable in a stripling but preposterous in a short-winded neurotic of forty-five?"

"Precisely," the conductor nodded, consulting his turnip. "If my calculations are correct, he has just finished his eleventh cigarette since retiring, verified his bank balance for the hundredth time, and is lapsing into a tortured doze. Give him the business." The engineer nodded. Three seconds later, the person they were discussing—and now I make bold to drop the domino: it was indeed myself—was catapulted violently upward in his bed. As my head caromed off the bed-lamp and struck the bridge of my daughter's 'cello, with which I was sharing the berth, the compartment was flooded with light and my wife's strained, anxious face came into view below.

"The Angostura!" she squealed. "Quick! It just fell into the sink!" No cardiac patient bereft of his digitalis could have packed quite as much anguish into so few syllables. Swinging from the berth with the grace of a kinkajou who has temporarily mislaid his eyeglasses, I seized a huck towel and neatly sopped up the precious lifegiving fluid, not forgetting to include several shards of glass. My movements, to be candid,

My movements, to be candid, were not aided materially by a torrent of salted nuts and fruits.

were not aided materially by a torrent of salted nuts and fruit which chose this moment to cascade from a bon voyage basket overhead, nor by the presence underfoot of five suitcases, a foot-locker, two flight bags, a portable apparatus for condensing drinking water, and an incomplete file of the minutes of the Royal Geographical Society.

"There now," I said cheerfully, rubbing a few bacilli into my lacerated palms to insure gangrene and shrewdly scanning the graying horizon. "We ought to be in Chicago before long. What do you say to a steaming dish of farina and some grilled kidneys?" My companion told me without hesitation what she would say, and lulled by the staccato rhythm of the square wheel directly beneath our heads, we sank into a refreshing slumber. Our eyelids had scarcely granulated before the unmistakable sound of children belaboring each other filtered through the door of the adjoining compartment. Four or five strokes of the cat, administered so as to stimulate circulation without actually breaching the skin, put the young into a more docile humor, and soon our foursome was seated in the diner. While waiting for coffee, the preparation of which consumed no more time than the reconstruction of the Portland Vase, I familiarized the fledglings with the locale outside, explaining the operation of the stockyards, the grain elevators, and the complex railways that make Chicago a hub. Luckily both youngsters were at that impressionable age—twelve and ten respectively—when childish curiosity knows no bounds.

Eyes round as saucers, they gave vent to repeated exclamations of wonder.

"Jiminy crickets!" breathed Adam in an awestruck voice. "Listen to the old *gephompheter* behind me work his false choppers!" The old *gephompheter*, a dropsical burgess patently on his way to Battle Creek for the waters, turned and favored him with a glance that was pure corrosive sublimate, but the lad refused to quail. "Hiya, fat stuff," he said easily. At that juncture, I realized with a start that I had neglected to wear my trousers into the diner, an oversight which afforded a good excuse to retire and take the boy with me. It is interesting to note that to this day, a full year and a half later, one of his earlobes is still over a centimeter longer than the other.

The Chicago stopover was brief, merely sufficient to heat the drinking water and sprinkle grit on the towels, but it enabled me to dash out and procure some Danish pastry, bananas, and popcorn. Frankly, I had become a trifle disturbed at the paucity of flies in our compartment; the careless shrug I received from the Pullman conductor when I complained convinced me I would have to remedy the situation myself. Although the cheese buns were not as sticky as I would have liked and the bananas were hardly overripe, we managed to make do. By Cedar Rapids, our quarters, while far from ideal, were in fairly adequate confusion. The seats were heaped with torn comic books, crossword puzzles, rubbers, playing cards, toothbrushes, and underclothes bulging from half-open satchels, and there was a mulch of luggage and food on the floor, pullulating with flies, that promised complete bedlam before Denver.

Of the dozen-odd transcontinental trips I have made in the past decade, the present was unquestionably the most circuitous. As nearly as I could ascertain, we reached San Francisco less by steering a westerly course than by closing in on it in decreasing circles. Every few hundred miles, our car was shunted onto a siding and attached to a railroad whose dining cars were even more unspeakable than the last. High in the list were the Chicago, Burlington & Quincy and the Denver, Rio Grande & Western; by exercising constant vigilance, their maîtres d'hôtel and waiters achieved a degree of insolence and incompetence unmatched outside Egypt. If no railroad was available at the moment, our sleeper was hooked to trolley cars, stagecoaches, wagon trains, pantechnicons, manure spreaders—anything that happened to be rolling in the general direction of the Bay City. With the Western Pacific, at Salt Lake, the picture altered for the better. Personnel and equipment were no longer medieval, and it was agreeable again to be treated as a traveler instead of a deportee. The Vista Dome car used on this system, incidentally, was a fairly unique experience. As one lolled in its rooftop observation blister, vacuously listening to Muzak recordings of Amy Woodford Finden in the intense sunlight, the effect was indistinguishable from a California cultist funeral. On the occasion I did so, I was privileged to overhear an elderly couple, who obviously had just met, absorbedly

discussing their internal functions. "I always keep reg-
ular with psyllium seed," she was saying. "It gives you
the bland bulk without any of the harsh abrasives."
"Ye-e-es, that's so," the old gentleman conceded mag-
nanimously, "but for day-in, day-out performance, for
real dependability, I like syrup of figs, with a good
alophen tablet in case of blockage." How fundamental,
so to speak, and how real, I reflected, as we whizzed
along the glorious Feather River Route at a mile a
minute. Here were two kinsprits, all passion spent,
meeting at last on a plane of perfect understanding.
Overcome with emotion, I swayed blindly downstairs
to the club car for a fast aperient.

*I was privileged to overhear a couple in the vista dome
engaged in a vital discussion.*

No band of Polish immigrants setting foot in the New World could have displayed quite so creamy a mélange of sullenness, martyrdom, and disillusion as my little troupe that winter morning aboard the Oakland ferry. Shivering in an icy rain amid our myriad traps, the ranee and the lambkins glowered at San Francisco and filed a long, sorrowful beef. "He said there were gonna be coconuts," ran the chant. "I wanna ride in a rickshaw. I feel like a frump in these clothes. I wanna ride in a pagoda. I wanna see a fight between a cobra. You deliberately made me buy all the wrong clothes so I'd look ridiculous. I wanna mango—he said there were gonna be mangoes. I wanna coke. I wanna hamburger. I wanna see Alcatraz."

"You'll see it soon enough," I promised, grinding my teeth to keep them warm. "Now look, where did you put those baggage checks they gave me in New York?"

"Why, in your trunk," my wife replied loftily. "You said to put them in a safe place."

"I know, angel," I said, opening a flange in my skull to allow the steam to escape, "but don't you see, if the checks are *inside,* the treeple won't give us the punk—I mean, the trunkle won't give us the peep——"

"Loosen his collar," I heard a faraway voice saying. "Stand back there—give him room!" The buzzing subsided and I found myself looking up into a circle of anxious faces. Within a half hour, thanks to my unusual restorative powers, I was coherent enough to intimate to my wife that since the trunks had been shipped directly to the S. S. *President Cleveland,* it would be difficult to gain access to them before leaving for Hollywood.

"Hollywood?" she demanded. "What do we have to go to Hollywood for? Is the ship sailing from there?" I slowly counted up to seventy-five to forestall a syncope and explained that inasmuch as the steamer was not scheduled to depart for Hong Kong for ten days, I thought the sprouts ought to get a hinge at the dream factory. Mollified by my assurances that she could spend money there as freely as in San Francisco, she grumbled assent and we made for the airport.

Winging over the Tehachapi Range, I prepared myself for the psychological climate of Los Angeles with a cursory inspection of its newspapers. It was reassuring to discover that the inmates assayed as high a percentage of helium as ever. The current suspect in the Black Dahlia case, a peccadillo which involved a lady of the evening being sawed into stove lengths, was described as studying to be a midget auto racer. An inventor in Palos Verdes had constructed a machine duplicating all the functions of the human brain. When not compounding interest or daydreaming about Billie Dove's shape, the mechanism lay by his fireside and purred like a cat. A group of taxpayers domiciled near a small training field in Burbank were up in arms. It appeared that the runway was adjacent to a disused cemetery and that when student pilots failed to become airborne fast enough, their planes plowed through the sepulchers, sending up a shower of knee-caps and femurs. Spurred on, no doubt, by the Southland's continual preoccupation with mortality, a local travel agency was advertising its facilities under the terse admonition, "See the World Before You Leave It."

Our entry into Los Angeles was fortuitously timed; the choking layer of smog which has earned the community the sobriquet of "The Pittsburgh of the West" was nowhere in evidence. However, the city was digging itself out of a snowfall that had attained a depth of three-quarters of an inch at some points, and emergency crews equipped with hot Sanka and soy-bean poultices were being rushed to the stricken area. Moving with its customary energy, the Chamber of Commerce issued a statement declaring the outrage to be Communist-inspired and posted a reward of ten thousand figs for the apprehension of the ringleaders. Nevertheless, it was not until Major Jack Warner had consulted a geomancer on Pico Boulevard and sacrificed three scenario writers to appease the elements that public confidence was finally restored.

As the parents of two passionate admirers of Lassie, the wonder collie, it was naturally our obligation to arrange a rendezvous with all possible speed. The meeting took place several days later on a sound stage at MGM, where the dog (who, parenthetically, is not a dog at all but a cunning simulacrum animated by two dwarf actors) was making a film about sheep-stealing in Scotland. Aquiver with anticipation, the children waited outside their idol's dressing room until he concluded a conference with his agent, business manager, and lawyer. At length the animal appeared, clad in smoking jacket and yellow Ascot muffler and puffing an imported shell briar. His manner, though cordial, was a whit abstracted; it was plain to see that he was dissatisfied with the script and felt that the writers had let him down. At a command from his handler, Lassie extended a languid, manicured paw to us all, wiped it fastidiously with a Kleenex, and strolled off. I inquired of the handler whether it was true as reported that his charge possessed almost human intelligence.

"He's the equal of any producer on this lot," he replied ambiguously. "Excuse me, but I have to go and see a dog about a man." On a near-by stage, a company was engaged in shooting *Madame Bovary*, Flaubert's classic, and we were permitted to watch Jennifer Jones acting the title role, an experience American moviegoers would be denied for many months to come. Appetites sharpened to the vanishing point, we now betook ourselves to the commissary, passing en route the Irving G. Thalberg Memorial Building, which houses most of the studio's executives and creative sparkplugs. It was in this noble structure, familiarly known as "The Iron Lung," that the memsahib and I had languished throughout a good part of the Thirties, and as our step quickened, we caught again the infallible fetor of balderdash, fatuity, and self-abasement that rises when the mountain labors to bring forth a scenario.

Reports had latterly been seeping across the snows of the Great Continental Divide that as a result of extensive legislative snooping, the film colony was racked by fear and espionage and that nobody dared express his political convictions. In the MGM commissary at least, one saw no hint of it. True, the chair I sat in had a dictaphone concealed under it and a man at the next table took down everything we said in shorthand, but all about us people spoke their minds in forthright fashion, seemingly oblivious of consequences. The names of Susan B. Anthony, Eugene Debs, and Samuel Gompers were bandied about on every lip, and one hothead, a partisan of Teddy Roosevelt, the Rough Rider, even undertook to applaud the latter's dictum of "Bust the Trusts." Midway in his panegyric, he suddenly became aware of Adam listening to him with open-mouthed interest.

"Who—who's that?" he quavered, springing to his feet and upsetting his yoghurt. I assured him it was only my son, but he was clearly unmanned. "He looks like an FBI agent to me," he muttered, sponging his forehead with a Q-tip. "Jeez, don't let this get any further. If Darryl or L.B. ever heard it, I'm out on my can."

The social life of the industry, into which we threw ourselves with the abandon of a couple of juniors home for the holidays from Miss Walker's School, had changed little in two years. It still consisted of an endless round of buffets full of people one had met the previous evening, all of them exactly one day older. Dinner-party conversation in a manufacturing center like Lowell, Nashua, or Wilmington usually deals with shoes, blankets, or smokeless powder, relieved with gossip about the foreman of the bleaching room niggling up to the stockroom babes. In Beverly Hills it dealt with previews, credits, and the boudoir escapades of any couple who had failed to attend that evening. Necks were engorged with blood and passions fanned to white heat as our screenwriter friends wrangled over their precise mathematical contributions to various current movies. "I did seventeen and one-fifth per cent of the original story idea of *Wizened!*" they shouted, "and thirty-two and five-sixteenths per cent of the additional dialogue of *He Shot Her Bolt!* Come on outside, you bastard!" Our impending voyage to the East was regarded with overwhelming envy. By turns each of the guests confessed to us that he would love to travel but the premiums on his annuities kept him in want. At the end of the meal, the ladies retired to their hostess's bedroom to compare handbags and hysterectomies, and the gentlemen, lighting cheroots, drank bumpers of Madeira to the *Wunderkind* of the week, typified at that point by Dore Schary. It was a piquant mixture of the Main Line, the Mermaid Tavern, and any lesser French penal colony like New Caledonia; and when, on the ninth day, we awoke with the characteristic roar in the antrums which betokens a surfeit of unreality, I knew it was time to load the felt yurts on the shaggy ponies and graze on.

Excitement was rife in the waiting room of the Los Angeles municipal airport as we straggled in. A mechanism similar to a jukebox, called the Insurograph and vending life insurance policies up to $25,000 at a quarter a throw, had recently been installed. Around it milled a dozen prospective air passengers, faces fever-flushed and chattering like ticket-holders at the Irish Sweepstakes. My attempt to curl up in a quiet corner with *Peekaboo,* a journal of the *haute poitrine* filled with angle shots of Dusty Anderson, came to naught; dragging me by the coattails, the children besought me to try my luck. Judging from the legend on the face of the Insurograph, "If good coin has been rejected, reinsert," parties unknown had already attempted to beat the machine. I fished a slug out of my change-purse and followed suit, but without success. After protracted bickering as to which portion of whom needed coverage most, I compromised by insuring my wallet, naming the Stuyvesant Cat Hospital beneficiary. Unfortunately for the grimalkins, who might today be rolling in salmon, our plane arrived in San Francisco in apple-pie order—a demonstration at once of the folly of gambling and of removing one's eyes for even an instant from Dusty Anderson.

In the monstrous clangor of the embarkation shed, jostled by porters trundling baggage trucks and deafened by the crash of cargo slings, we stared mutely at the *President Cleveland* towering above us. Throughout the next few weeks, until it deposited us on an alien shore to become targets for malaria, dysentery, Singapore foot, bilharzia, frambesia, sprue, Delhi boils, tropical ulcers, monkey pox, dengue fever, predatory shopkeepers, and *Heimweh,* this gleaming gray levia-

*A mechanism similar to a jukebox, vending insurance
at a quarter a throw.*

than would be home. For the children it was a challenge, the largest single object they had ever been called upon to take apart. To my wife, it was the opportunity she had been thirsting for, a chance to unpack her effects and scramble them so they could never be repacked. To me it was a peaceful haven between worlds, beyond the jangle of the telephone, where I could tot up the bills I owed and worry myself into neurasthenia.

"Well, folks," I said in what began as a portentous baritone and ended as a falsetto trill. *"Les jeux sont faits.* Cast off."

"What's the matter?" my wife queried, with that devilish intuition her sex betrays on the most infelicitous occasions. "Getting cold feet?"

"Listen, you," I said, my eyes as pitiless as flint. "Once I set my hand to the plow——" Exactly what dread events transpired when I did so, she never found out, for the rest of the sentence was blasted into eternity by the bellow of the ship's siren. My wife sighed deeply, shook her head, and trudged after me up the gangplank.

"Move over, Asia," she said compassionately. "Poor old continent. You don't know what's coming at you."

The largest single object our children had ever been called upon to take apart.

3

The Wild Blue Yonder

I F BY SOME odd quirk of circumstance you had happened to be an albatross, booby, or kestrel on the morning of January 23, 1949, winging on graceful pinions west of the Farallones, you might have descried out of your wicked little red-rimmed eyes a white pinpoint on the horizon. Inquisitively wheeling closer on the chance that it might be other boobies, you would have been chopfallen to discern a trim gray vessel of approximately twenty-three thousand gross registered tons, steaming S.S.W. on the Great Circle route from

San Francisco to Hong Kong and swiftly bearing six hundred escapists beyond the reach of Milton Berle and the National Retail Credit Association. Unless you were inherently a masochist, one glance at the passengers would have satisfied your curiosity. On the boat deck far below there would have been visible twenty or thirty retired wowsers in flowered lanai shirts and Lundberg caps, variously engaged in honeycombing their livers with bourbon, tickling skittish widows and cheating each other at shuffleboard, and reviling the Securities and Exchange Commission. The juxtaposition of their fuchsia-colored phizzes and the implausible turquoise sky, of the dazzling white superstructure and the emerald sea, would have produced an effect strikingly akin to a Kodachrome off register; and feathers screaming, you would have gone into a steep bank and made for Pitcairn with the conviction that you had had a pretty narrow squeak.

Overlooked in your quick scrutiny of the *President Cleveland,* however, there would have been one emigrant whose *savoir-vivre* and Apollo-like fairness set him as far apart from his fellows as Spinoza from a swineherd. Blessed with a disposition as tractable as a cougar's, possessed of the rare ability to comprehend only that which redounded to his own advantage, he had literally lifted himself to insignificance by his own bootstraps. From every fold of his radiant, saintly face (which by another odd quirk of circumstance happened to be my own), shone forth the man's passionate credo: take nothing but what is not actually nailed down. As he perched on a stool in the Hurricane Bar, pensively sipping his apéritif and appraising his features in a small hand-mirror, he knew a moment of deep melancholy. What a chasm separated him from the trivial, shallow creatures about him, he thought sadly. Would it ever be possible to bridge the gulf, to free these poor blind grubs from their cocoons and aid them to soar with him onto the astral plane? I had had several ponies of Reckitt's Blue and was feeling tolerably well starched when my wife entered, rudely short-circuiting my reverie. She exuded the special aura of triumph women display after spending several hundred dollars of other people's savings at the hairdresser's, and her coiffure, each serpent tightly finger-waved, fairly gleamed.

"Here's a cable for you, bub," she said pompously. While I busied myself opening it—I was at the stage where envelope flaps showed a tendency to fight me— she apprised me of an announcement on the loudspeaker that all passengers would be retarded as the ship proceeded westward.

"Hm-m-m, I thought they had reached their nadir," I commented. "Hot ziggety—what's this?"

"Good news, dear?" she asked eagerly.

"Wait till you hear," I chortled. "Remember that tiresome old barn of ours in the country we remodeled into a playroom at ruinous expense? Well, it seems that your nephew was fooling with some matches and now we have space for the tennis court I've always dreamed of."

"Yes, and think of all the charcoal we'll have for our wienie roasts in future," she agreed joyously. A tiny cloud momentarily overshadowed her even tinier face. "I do wish it could have been one of our children who was responsible. They never seem to have any enterprise."

"There, there," I consoled her. "They'll be just as toxic as that big lunkhead after they've lived in the Orient. Where are they, by the way?" A hasty catechism of the deck stewards revealed that Abby was dealing fan-tan with three Chinese bust-out men in the cardroom, while Adam, assisted by another supercharged delinquent, had tied up Sparks and was sending out distress signals to the Asiatic Squadron. Reminded by the cool liquid notes of the luncheon gong that I had taken on no cool liquids for almost five minutes, I rectified the oversight and we joined the other colorfully clad tax evaders streaming down for their midday carbohydrates.

The décor of the *President Cleveland* had little in common with that of the ocean greyhounds we remembered from the early Thirties, nor, indeed, with any recognizable nautical tradition. Industrial designers and interior decorators had blown their tops, investing her public rooms with a profusion of monel metal, formica and glass plastics, and splashy murals depicting generously endowed nereids sporting among the billows with dolphins. Through those refined and ruthlessly air-conditioned precincts moved phalanxes of cat-footed waiters dedicated to anticipating your

*Six hundred escapists beyond the reach of Milton Berle
and the National Retail Credit Association.*

every wish. It was overpoweringly functional and as hygienic as a brain clinic, but every so often you felt a catch in your throat at the memory of those antebellum French cabin boats, with their matchless bouquet of lavabo, spilt Pinard, hot salt water, and garlic.

Once the napkin was furled under the jowls and you started tucking in the groceries, though, nostalgia died like a dog. The barrage of vittles that bombarded the *President Cleveland's* passengers on her sixth Pacific crossing was indescribable; the closest analogy I can offer is the Homeric fodder the Hoosiers were wont to stow away in Indiana at the turn of the century, as described by George Ade in his immortal "Fable of the Waistband That Was Taut Up Till the Moment It Gave Way." The chief steward apparently felt that unless every man jack of us was carried groaning with heartburn from the table, mutiny would sweep the ship. To this end he plied us at each meal with eighteen or twenty recherché appetizers like caviar, herring filets, soused mackerel, North Sea sprats, cracked crab, sardellen, and Philadelphia head cheese; an array of soups, broths, and bisques distilled from every crustacean, fowl, and quadruped ever classified by Buffon; fish snared the width and breadth of the Seven Seas; eggs and rarebits innumerable; entrees employing the flesh not only of common edible animals but of bears, wolves, stags, boars, hartebeests, springboks, and wapiti; cold buffets and salads of endless variety and ingenuity; and sweetmeats, savories, and cheeses that made the head ring with their succulence and scope. Personally, I am an ascetic type boy; just give me a soupçon of pâté de foie gras, a cup of vichyssoise, a filet of Dover sole, a small entrecôte about the size of a longshoreman's hand flanked by potatoes Anna and hothouse peas, a galantine of capon in spiced jelly, a mixed green salad, a pot de crème au chocolat, a few fragments of Pont l'Évêque, and a touch of Brazilian coffee—give me little else, I repeat, and I can curl up on the bare floor with my tartan wrapped around me. But I do think there is no more appalling sight than people stuffing themsevles indiscriminately, and there were times in that dining saloon, particularly after I had finished eating, when the gluttony of my neighbors forced me to avert my eyes.

One of the worst offenders, though it costs me an effort to confess it, was my own good lady, who was frequently to be observed recumbent in a deck-chair following these debauches, peepers as heavy-lidded as a constrictor who has just engorged a chicken. I would chide her lightly, throwing in joking allusions to Kate Smith and the three-toed sloth, but no entreaty could dissipate her lethargy. As a result, I was invariably forced to interrupt work I should have been doing, such as reading aloud extracts from the Kamasutra to an inconsolable divorcee behind a lifeboat, and go below to supervise the children's lessons. Our initial sessions, truthfully, were none too rewarding. The bulk of the problems in their arithmetic dealt with an unattractive dullard named Farmer Brown who had cut up his lower forty into rhomboids or isosceles triangles and was unable to compute the square of the hypotenuse. After breaking my nails on his dilemma, I explained to the cubs that if, instead of mousing around with Euclid, Brown would set out a little marijuana in his fields, he could check both erosion and foreclosure. Rather than rehash poppycock of no conceivable use in Southeast Asia, I got down to brass tacks. With the aid of a blanket and Nick Scarne's admirable treatise on dice, I gave the young a bit of instruction in calculating odds, fading, and supplicating the bones. I also taught them a few simple methods of smuggling contraband past customs officials, the technique of haggling with pedicab drivers and rickshaw men, and the minimum provocation needed to kick or cuff one's native boys. We concluded with several rudimentary exercises in black market manipulation, at which they showed an adroitness and chicanery that would have shamed a weasel. I could not help but feel a glow of fatherly pride subsequently in Hong Kong when I met them skulking along Ice House Street, pockets stuffed with rupees, Straits dollars, and Indonesian guilders, for I knew that at last my drudgery had borne fruit.

Five days after we had slid through the Golden Gate, the ship rounded Diamond Head and there ensued a feverish twelve-hour kaleidoscope of paper leis, tanned Miami bail-jumpers chanting spurious Hawaiian *Lieder*, and raw fish drowned in a species of library paste called poi. Bowed under armloads of tin ukuleles and promotional literature lavished on us by the Chamber of Commerce, we parked the striplings at the Outrigger Canoe Club with orders to acquire a second-degree burn and canvassed the shops of Waikiki Beach. The boast that they contain the world's most hideous curios is, in my opinion, pure chauvinism. True, they have managed to torture rattan, clay, and sea-shells into some extraordinarily repellent knick knacks, but I saw nothing even remotely as emetic as the worry-birds and musical toilets of my own Sixth Avenue. The afternoon was marred by only one slight contretemps. We were just leaving Gump's, where my wife had spent an hour cooing over that shop's collection of coral and spinach jade, when Mr. Richard Gump breathlessly overtook us. With some concern, he called attention to an angry swelling in my breast-pocket, offering to summon medical assistance if necessary. I pooh-poohed his anxiety, supposing it to be merely a hernia induced by overexertion. What was our surprise, therefore, to discover that a Han jade cup, formerly the property of the Dowager Empress of China, had fallen into my clothes unbeknownst to me. As soon as the mystery was cleared up, we all enjoyed a hearty chuckle at Gump's expense and he conducted us back to the dock personally to make sure we had incurred no untoward effects from our visit.

By mid-Pacific the tropical heat had wrought a subtle transformation aboardship; the officers blossomed out in whites, passengers sorted themselves into practical jokers, self-made men, close personal friends of Mr. MacArthur, and similar bores, and a spirit of merrymaking as uncompromising as that of the borscht circuit made itself manifest. Every evening vast, frenzied cocktail parties raged in the Bubbling Well Bar, tendered by salvage tycoons and kittenish Southern harridans ablaze with diamonds. At mealtimes the public address system was constantly warbling "Happy Birthday to You" to signalize the imminence of senility, and august executives in paper hats and rompers capered grimly through the passageways, braying on horns. It was a time to try men's souls.

To what degree the destruction of Manila and the anguish her inhabitants had endured shook the equilibrium of some of our fellow travelers was made clear soon after our arrival there. "Do you know what I had to pay for a box of beauty clay here?" I heard an elderly dragon with a resurrected face indignantly demand of her companion. "Three pesos—a dollar-fifty! Why, you can get the same thing in Grosse Pointe for forty cents!" The other Eumenides hissed sympathetically. "It's a scandal," one assented, "and can you imagine living in all that rubble the way they do? Not an ounce of self-respect." Several other disgruntled observers, whose cabs had been delayed in traffic on the Escolta owing to reconstruction, surmised that granting the islands their independence had caused the mischief. The Filipinos were not ready for it, they declared sagely. Inevitably, of course, and by that nimble club-car ratiocination in which the upper brackets engage at the drop of a bond, the true culprit stood revealed—Franklin Delano Roosevelt. The Great Be-

"Do you know what I had to pay
for a box of beauty clay here?"

trayer, working with his Red cohorts in the unions, had shackled free enterprise, deflowered the American Way, and reduced us to the status of witless helots. Now, had Dewey been elected . . . Their shoulders were racked with dry sobs.

It demands hair-trigger caution on a transpacific cruise, not to say the reflexes of a circus aerialist, to dodge the sightseeing which becomes epidemic the moment the ship touches port. Before the screw has quite stopped revolving, busloads of tourists begin disappearing into the scrub to eavesdrop on some rachitic aborigine at his vespers or gape at the headstone of a forgotten conquistador. At Manila, while we managed to by-pass the usual shrines, dungeons, and fortifications, we were cozened into visiting a cigar factory, an experience which for sheer ennui transcends even the vaudeville turn of Benny Fields. It took a sizable number of gimlets and a trip to the Miramar, the *boîte de nuit* favored of the moment, to dispel the effects. Anybody interested in ravishing women—not in the Sabine sense, purely in viewing some exquisite lassies—will find his sensibilities agreeably teased there. The dance floor swarmed with enchanting young Filipinas who wore the transparent puff sleeves of piña cloth characteristic of the locale and danced the *paso doble* with the verve of Argentinita. At the invitation of the manager, a sinister bonze straight out of Raymond Chandler sporting a mouthful of gold teeth, we passed an instructive hour in his gambling rooms overhead. I was amused to hear how quickly word spread that I had

A quartet of foreign devils
manifestly aching to be plundered.

entered the establishment; the croupiers were taut with expectancy and on every hand I heard awed whispers of "There's the man who took the Greek Syndicate at Monte Carlo two years ago!" Their apprehensiveness, however, was unwarranted. I was in no mood for play, and except for the trifling three or four thousand I negligently staked to humor my wife, stifling a yawn the while, I was richly content to study the passing scene. I had just become engrossed in studying a shapely, sloe-eyed mestiza with flowerlike hands who was dealing blackjack when the mem decided my eyes were overstrained and, grasping me firmly by the scruff, catapulted me into a droshky.

Amid a cataclysmic downpour that drummed against her ports like hail, the *President Cleveland* moved at long last into the harbor of Hong Kong. Narrowly missing Victoria and the Peak, shrouded in fog, the ship swung into its berth at Kowloon guided by the pilot and captain alone, for I was far too busy stealing pillowcases to give them the assistance they clamored for. Eleven coolies in massive capes woven of rushes bore our baggage to the customs shed; in a lather of hysteria, scattering cumshaw about me like grain, I deposited in a bonded godown the hundred cartons of cigarettes I had laid by for emergencies ahead. Within a couple of hours, His Britannic Majesty's watchdogs had assured themselves that our gear contained no firearms, gold, or opium, and we were afloat again. The ancient, leaky wallah-wallah bearing us to

Hong Kong Island was almost scuppers awash under our luggage; bailing like madmen, soaked to the skin, the four of us beseeched the boatmen to pull for the distant shore. The little craft rose, fell, and rose again, and for a horrid instant I feared we were all fore-doomed to Davy Jones's locker. Then I dauntlessly brushed the rain from my face, encircled my wife's waist, and spoke the words that give a woman the courage to go on.

"You got me into this rat race, sweetheart," I said. "I'll never forget as long as I live." A few simple words, and yet they gave her the stability she lacked. I saw her lips frame the phrase, "You utter, utter darling," but she was too moved to pronounce it. And so, hand in hand and neck in noose, we rode forward into the promise of a new dawn.

The ancient, leaky Wallah-Wallah
was almost scuppers awash.

4

Mama Don't Want No Rice

O N A DANK WINTER'S day shortly after the
Chinese New Year, the population of Upper Lascar
Row in Hong Kong was enjoying its midmorning snack
of bêche-de-mer and jasmine tea when the street was
galvanized by the advent of a quartet of foreign devils
so manifestly aching to be plundered that a mighty
hosanna welled up the length of Queen's Road Central.
Abacuses began clicking furiously, catchpenny ivories
of the goddess Kwan Yin bloomed on every curio
dealer's shelf, factory-fresh Ming horses were hastily

baptized with dust to simulate age and tempting whiffs of Lapsang Soochong wafted about to decoy the Outer Barbarians. While the latter bore no placard proclaiming their nationality, certain obscure indications tended to establish them as an American family. In typically Yankee matriarchal style, the party was headed by a well-preserved woman of thirty-odd, her features distorted by an insensate craving for bargains and an iron resolve to paper the Thieves' Market with her husband's money. Trotting at her heels, as obedient as a coach-dog, came the present deponent, bearing in his arms the gallimaufry of opium lamps, snuff-bottles, door-knockers, sandalwood fans, and ceremonial scrolls she had bartered for his heart's blood. A man of rare gentleness, possessed of almost Socratic wisdom and a patience outrivaling Job's, he recognized no law but his wife's airy caprice; at her bidding (provided, of course, that he was not otherwise occupied), he was prepared to scale the snows of Everest or plumb deepest Lake Titicaca. Straggling behind and alternately whining, sassing their parents, and cudgeling each other, there followed two wiry hooligans in levis and polychromatic flannel jumpers. It was a sight for sore eyes, this close-knit, harmonious little company sprinkling valuta indiscriminately over the crown colony, and many miraculous cures were subsequently reported by local opticians. The day dawns, nevertheless, when even the Comstock Lode yields up nothing but gravel, and finally, on the very brink of insolvency, I brought the juggernaut to a halt. Straining at a gnat and swallowing the smoke of a Camel, I slapped from my wife's hand the Sung pipkin she had purchased with our last greenback.

"That's enough rubbish for one day, sweetheart," I hinted. "Back to the carbarn before I touch a whip to your flanks." My sally, as I anticipated, awoke no response from the stolid creature, whose sense of humor seldom rose above the Punch and Judy level. Flushed with resentment, eyes akimbo, she planted herself squarely in my path and declined to move. Fortunately, I happened to recall an apothegm of the T'ang dynasty to the effect that more flies may be captured with honey than with vinegar. I adroitly introduced the subject of food and suggested that we have a spot of tiffin in a tiny Szechuanese restaurant near by, where the sweet-and-sour squid and *gedämpfte* kelp boasted an international reputation.

"I refuse to taste another spoonful of that excelsior!" announced the margravine in a ringing voice. "We've been on this blasted reef four days and all we've eaten is barnacles and boiled string! I want something that sticks to the ribs."

"Hamburgers!" the children caught up her refrain. "We want flapjacks with maple syrup—chicken enchiladas—apple pandowdy!" By now a crowd of several hundred Chinese was pressing in on us, eager to miss none of the fireworks; so, distributing to them a rough translation of the proceedings in the Fukien dialect, concluding with an impassioned appeal never to marry, never to have children, and never to travel abroad with their wives and children, I made our adieux. We dined sumptuously on triple-decker sandwiches and quadruple malteds at a busy soda fountain off Chater Road, whose neon lighting and ulcerous tempo afforded a reasonably repugnant facsimile of our neighborhood drugstore. Over the postprandial Bisodol tablet, I bade my bride close her eyes and placed in her outstretched palm a bulky envelope. Her wee brow wrinkled in perplexity as she spelt out the destination of the steamer tickets within.

"What's this?" she asked suspiciously. "Why does it stand 'Macassar' on these?"

"Because that's where the steamer goes, honey," I smiled. "It's the principal port on the island of Celebes."

"Is that anywhere near Bangkok?" she demanded. "Come on, answer me—none of that Eric Ambler stuff!"

"Well—er—vaguely," I hedged. "About twenty-seven hundred miles as the crow flies, more or less. Naturally, we won't——"

"Just a second, Jocko," she interrupted, quivering with anger. "Do I interpret this to mean that you inveigled me all the way to Siam and then switched the deck on us?"

"Of course not," I said placatingly. "It's a little extra dividend—kind of a warm-up for Siam, so to speak. By the time you get back from the Moluccas—if you ever *do* come back—Siam will look like Rockefeller Plaza." Exactly as instinct had warned me, the poor thing kicked up the most preposterous fuss. She drew a ghoulish picture of a remote and unexplored archipelago swarming with vampire bats, anthropophagi, and virulent diseases; cited some absurd fiddle-faddle about the war in Java (a grotesque designation for the minor police action in which the Dutch, to preserve order, had unavoidably bombed Djokjakarta and were being forced to kill a few thousand extremists); and having pilloried me as irresponsible, a delayed juvenile, and an erotic dreamer nourished on *Terry and the Pirates,* flung her arms around the children and defied Lucifer himself to drag her to the East Indies. To overcome such a hash of obscurantism and prejudice was a task calculated to intimidate a lesser man, but I flatter myself I brought it off rather well. Tapping a monogrammed Zira on the wafer-thin, solid gold cigarette case conferred on me by the Sublime Porte in connection with certain trifling services in the matter of the Missing Halvah, I pointed out with a silky smile that through a freak of bookkeeping, I alone was privileged to endorse our express cheques, which gave me what is known in sporting circles as an edge. "Do you not think, *cara mia,*" I pursued, "that, though undeniably colorful and renowned for its hospitality, Hong Kong would not be the most ideal place for an attractive matron—who, parenthetically, is not getting any younger—and two helpless minors to go on the beach? I ask this, mind you, in an altogether objective spirit, knowing that your opinion will be couched likewise."

"You rat," replied my wife, employing a pet name

she had found useful in domestic crises when logic failed. It being self-evident that she should never have crossed foils with so superior an adversary, I gallantly forgave her temerity and proceeded to outline our itinerary: two weeks' voyage aboard the M/s *Kochleffel* along the periphery of Java via the South China Sea, calling at Batavia, Semarang, and Surabaya, and thence northward to Macassar. "What happens there?" she asked wearily, a look of dumb resignation investing her face. "I suppose we all remove our drawers and plunge into the canebrake."

"In the hands of Disraeli, irony can be a formidable weapon," I rejoined. "In a lout it becomes merely offensive. At Macassar we transfer to the *Cinnabar*, a snug little coaster in the interisland copra trade, which will convey us to Pare-Pare, Donggala, Menado, Ternate, Morotai, Sorong (the westernmost tip of New Guinea), Batjan, and Amboina—in short, a sketchy circumnavigation of Celebes and the historic Spice Islands. I also plan, if the changing monsoon permits, to pay a visit to Banda Neira, that celebrated outpost of the Dutch nutmeg trade."

"There must be a gimmick in all this," she observed, moodily gnawing a piece of stem ginger. "In twenty years I have yet to detect you in a disinterested act."

"There is," I acknowledged. "The terminal point for our soiled laundry will be that jewel of the Lesser Sundas, the island of Bali."

"Aha!" she exclaimed triumphantly. "Everything falls into place. I was puzzled by the goatish gleam in your eye, but now I'm tuned in."

"The terminal point for our soiled laundry
will be Bali," I announced masterfully.

"Are you implying by any chance, madam," I asked scathingly, "that I would deliberately haul three persons on a five-thousand-mile journey through swamp and mangrove just to catch a glimpse of a bunch of superbly formed, mocha-colored young women in their nether garments? Because if you are," I said, rising haughtily, "I have nothing more to say."

"That," she said succinctly, "will be a relief all around—eh, kids?" The children's reply was inaudible, mainly because they had taken a powder during our tête-à-tête and made a beeline for Pedder Street, the informal bourse of Hong Kong. On being coralled outside the Swatow Lace Store, they disclosed a flimflam worthy of Ponzi, having thimblerigged the money-changers with a dizzying parlay of soap wrappers into Portuguese escudos into Singapore dollars. I could not bring myself to reprove them, particularly since they had cleared a tidy profit, but as a lesson to cut me into their grift in future, I made them finance a tour of the Tiger Balm Gardens at Causeway Bay.

This curious nonesuch, a conceit of Aw Boon Haw, the noted patent-medicine taipan and philanthropist, beggars description; it is at once a potpourri of Madame Tussaud's waxworks, the castle of Otranto, and a theatrical prop shop, the whole tinctured with fumes of the Mexican drug called mescal. Just what its eighteen acres of nightmare statuary, turrets, grottoes, mazes, and cloud-borne pagodas signify, nobody on earth knows—not even its proud parent, upon whom I called for a fast exegesis next morning at his headquarters in Wanchai Road. Prior to our interview, Mr.

MAMA DON'T WANT NO RICE

Haw's interpreter, a Celestial version of Russell Bird-
well, coated me with the customary schmaltz about
his employer's humble origins, business genius, and
benevolence. He then expanded with equal tedium on
the virtues of Tiger Balm itself, which he unhesi-
tatingly hailed as a specific for everything from St.
Anthony's fire to milk leg. Apparently this was the
universal belief, for I afterward observed Chinese air
passengers rubbing it on their foreheads to forestall air-
sickness, at the same time smearing it furtively on the
fuselage to insure the plane's staying aloft. For a preparation consisting largely of menthol and balsam, it
undoubtedly has extraordinary powers. They may de-
rive from Mr. Haw himself, a mettlesome old party in
carpet slippers, who gripped my hand with such extraordinary vigor that I was forced whimpering to my
knees.

"Now exactly what do you wish to know?" the interpreter began. Feeling that some preamble was required, I teed off with salutations from several American mandarins of comparable importance—Eugene S.
Grace, Lee Shubert, and the chairman of the New
York State Boxing Commission.

"In a few badly chosen words, how would you sum
up the theme of the Tiger Balm Gardens?" I inquired.

"Mr. Haw has presented to various hospitals and
deserving charities an amount in excess of eighteen
million Hong Kong dollars," replied the spokesman.
"He is a beloved figure, asking nothing for himself but
the right to serve his fellow man."

"He exudes an aura of goodness," I agreed courteously, cracking a sunflower seed between my mandibles, "but to return to the meaning of the Gardens. I sensed a definite surrealist influence, as though Max Ernst and the St. Louis Cardinals had collaborated on their design."

"The purely material is no longer of any consequence to Mr. Haw," the interpreter explained. "Spiritual salvation alone can save mankind from the abyss, as he points out in today's editorial in his three Chinese-language newspapers."

"I am hastening home to read it," I assured him. "But before I do, may I be allowed to put one more query?"

"What is that?"

"Has Mr. Haw given any inkling yet as to who will inherit his moola? If not, I should like to include my name among the legatees."

"I am afraid there is a fundamental cleavage between the East and the West," apologized the subordinate. "This way to your rickshaw, please." Nevertheless, as I bowled back to the Repulse Bay Hotel, gently flicking the coolie with a switch to ward off the flies, the audience did not seem wholly without benefit. It had given me an insight into the complexities of the Oriental mind such as one never gets from the sixty-five-cent luncheon at Chin Lee's and it had enabled the family in my absence to dream up a brand-new batch of complaints.

The most grievous, predictably, came from the missy, who was loud in her accusations that I had withheld

her from the night life of Hong Kong. "What did I
pack my evening dresses for, to wear in a Malay
prahu?" she blubbered. "If I were Alexis Smith you'd
be in a cummerbund fast enough." She contemptuously
brushed aside my protest that Catteraugus, New York,
was more diverting by far; she knew all about the evil
waterfront haunts, the swarthy lascars, and the Eurasian adventuresses from the novels of Achmed Ab-
dullah. The upshot was that at midnight we found ourselves in a titanic, murky cabaret almost devoid of
heat and customers, watching the only untalented
Negro in the world execute a cakewalk to the music
of a Filipino fife and drum corps. At its conclusion, as
though my hair was not sufficiently streaked with silver, he broke into "Mammy's Little Coal Black Rose."
I pushed away the plate of stone-cold spaghetti and
signaled to the waiter.

"Bring me a check and a steel-blue automatic," I
directed. My wife plucked at my sleeve, but I ignored
her. "Also, please ask that minstrel to wait for me in
his dressing room."

"Listen," she said insistently, "some people in that
corner are waving at you." The arrivals proved to be
an old college classmate now in the consular service
and two extremely decorative chickadees, from Canton
and Outer Mongolia respectively. A coalition was quickly arranged, half a dozen bottles of Polish vodka bur-
geoned from the tablecloth, and in a trice we were
yoked in close harmony, warbling "Brunonia, Mother
of Men" in pidgin. Before long a pair of laughing al-

mond eyes cajoled me to the dance floor, where my 1922-vintage toddle excited wide admiration, especially from those who had never seen a man dancing with a pair of laughing almond eyes. I had just consented after considerable suasion to call on the fair Tartar some afternoon and inspect a rare old sheepskin which had been in her family since the reign of Kublai Khan when my wife was stricken with one of her infrequent migraine headaches. There was no possible remedy but to frog-march me into a cab, drive to the hotel, and bind my hands to the bedpost with a sheet. This relieved her suffering somewhat, and soon the only sound in the corridor was her uneven breathing, interspersed with maledictions I had not dreamt she possessed.

Three days later, in a freezing wind that turned our noses blue with cold, we swayed up the accommodation ladder of the *Kochleffel*, buffeted by coolies groaning under our trunks. The harbor traffic flowed on briskly around the ship, oblivious of the importance of the occasion; toplofty little steamers bound for Macao rocked up-river, Kowloon-side ferries scraped past the bows, and quaint junks wallowed by, laden with Parker pens, self-winding Rolexes, and other imports vital to China's existence. Free of her buoy at last, the vessel moved at half speed past the bare brown hills; the last cluster of government buildings dropped astern, and we were at sea. Already the bar had begun to echo with guttural commands of "*Jonges!* Bring me here a Bols!" and toasts to Wilhelmina. Knocking the embers from my pipe into a lifeboat to prevent their

A pair of laughing almond eyes
cajoled me onto the dance floor.

scattering, I descended to our cabins. My three companions sat in the quickening gloom amid jumbled suitcases. It was obvious that their moral barometer was falling fast.

"Chin up, friends!" I adjured them jovially. "Before you know it, you'll be in Java."

"And that's practically home," added my wife in a lifeless voice. She rose and stared thoughtfully out the porthole. "Did I ever tell you," she went on, "that in order to marry you, I jilted an explorer?"

"Honestly?" I asked. "What did you tell him?"

"I wish I could remember," she murmured. "It sure would come in handy."

5

Columbia, the Crumb of the Ocean

O<small>F ALL THE SORRY</small> places on earth one might have elected to be caught in that February forenoon, it seemed to me that mine was easily the most wretched. To recline at full length in a wicker chair three miles off the coast of Borneo, shielded from the tropical sun by a snowy ship's awning and caressed by the vagrant airs of the west monsoon, and, between cooling draughts of lime squash tempered with a little gin, to contemplate the plight of my friends in New York, was as painful an experience as any I had ever endured. I pictured them drearily slogging through the blackened midwinter slush on sleeveless errands, hunched over their desks falsifying Hooper ratings and evolving new catch-phrases to sell merchandise nobody wanted, writing music that would never be hummed and novels that would be remaindered on publication day. I saw them, faces taut with nervous tension, bolting their food in the rough and tumble of crowded restaurants, having their pants pressed by dollar cleaners, teeth drilled by painless dentists, psyches purged by cut-rate analysts. My heart bled for them. With every fiber of my being I longed to be at their side, making their burden a little heavier and lending a deaf ear to their troubles, but unfortunately I was ten thousand miles away and getting farther every minute. Was there not some way I could pay tribute from this distant clime to their bulldog fortitude? I racked my brain without success, and then, of a sudden, it came to me. Touching the bell at my elbow I had had installed by a cunning artificer in Hong Kong, I instructed the Chinese bar steward to replenish my drink with three more. I was not actually drinking them for my own sake, I explained, but rather for my friends *in absentia*. He understood immediately (the Chinese have a quick awareness of the obligations of friendship), and sped away like the wind. I sighed contentedly and lay back, watching the milky jade wake of the vessel bubble astern as her mighty engines churned on toward the Indies.

Though scarcely seventy-two hours had elapsed since I had embarked my troupe on the *Kochleffel* for Batavia, I already felt a not inconsiderable affection for the ship. A stubby, comfortable packet built in the early Twenties for the Java-China-Japan service, her mahogany panels and brass fittings somehow reminded me of the old Fall River Line; I had the same exhilarating sense of sin and derring-do I had known in youth making a first overnight excursion from Providence to New York. What was sadly lacking, to be sure, was a couple of those raucous, scarlet-faced drummers smoking Hoffman Fancy Tales and bragging about their amorous triumphs, but at least we had an exotic equivalent in the two dozen Chinese émigrés from Amoy sharing first class with us. A number of these were dispersed about the deck at the moment, lapping up the ubiquitous orange soda of the East and dandling those extraordinary fat and cheerful infants characteristic of Chinese families on every economic level. Thirty feet off, my own larvae, puffy with sunburn, were absorbed in a cutthroat game of deck golf with Mynheer Vogt-Bensdorp, an elephantine Dutch lawyer from Java, and his equally massive vrouw. It was a gay and heart-warming scene, especially viewed through the hazy perspective of several toddies, and I was just falling into a divine snooze when my wife, with a woman's unfailing flair for disrupting her husband's well-being, erupted from a gangway. She leaned coquettishly on the arm of the captain, a Teutonic, bot-

She leaned coquettishly on the arm of the captain.

tle-nosed Hollander who had clearly just finished paying her some heavy gallantry, and the simper on their faces as they bore down on me was alarmingly like that of Kay Francis and Paul Henreid in a short-budget domestic comedy.

"Why, *there* you are, darling," she drawled with the same aristocratic hauteur Maggie was wont to assume toward Jiggs when she discovered his stockinged feet on the Chippendale. "Whatever are you doing with all those glasses?"

"Draining 'em," I replied tersely. "The same thing you were doing up in the chartroom when I peeked in a while ago."

"Oh, that," she smiled carelessly. "Captain van Popinjay was explaining the sextant to me, weren't you, captain?"

"I bet he was," I said. "With his arm around you to steady you against the roll of the ship. I don't know what we need a gyroscope for, the way this salt-water mink goes around steadying passengers against the roll of the ship."

"Please?" said the captain blandly. "I do not believe I understand very well."

"You're doing all right, Casanova," I growled. "Just keep those flippers of yours in the wheelhouse where they belong, *compisco?*" My spouse intervened nervously, knowing that if my ire were sufficiently aroused, I could demolish a grape with a single blow of my fist, and we adjourned to the veranda for the customary pre-luncheon ritual.

73

This institution, a sacrament aboard every Dutch cockleshell since the reign of William of Orange, was religiously attended by the entire Occidental contingent of nine, including the chief mate and the engineer, a young missionary of some obscure order bound for Flores, and a stolid housewife, heavily *enceinte,* who rarely lifted her eyes from her embroidery hoop. The routine was unvarying; we all sat rigidly upright in a circle gulping down countless ponies of Bols while our shipmates dredged up as many insults to America as they could think of. To describe in a paragraph the scope and malignity of their hatred would be impossible; suffice to say it took every form from mere boorishness to almost psychotic malevolence. Faced with the realization that their colonial empire was coming apart at the seams like a wet paper box, that after three centuries of befriending the Asiatic brother, their noses were being plucked out of the feedbag, and that their homeland within a few years must again shrink to an insignificant pimple on the North Sea, our Dutch cousins were in a truly fearful wax. By some nightmarish process of logic, they had succeeded in convincing themselves that the UNO was responsible for their debacle in Indonesia, and hence that we, as American nationals, were legitimate targets for their barbs. As we joined the *Kaffeeklatsch,* Father de Groot, the young missionary, favored us with a dazzling smile.

"I was just telling my countrymen," he said, "that if it were not for Hendrick Hudson, you Yankees would

74

still be eating dried buffalo meat and scalping each other."

"Yes, and don't forget Peter Stuyvesant, and Cornelius Vanderbilt," chimed in the chief engineer. "They civilized the barbarians and now the dirty money-grubbers are telling us how to rule our own subjects."

"Well, of course the Americans are not really civilized," observed Mynheer Vogt-Bensdorp, drawing comfortably on his perfecto. "Gangsters—assassins. Do you know that it is not safe for a girl to go out on the streets of Chicago?"

"Personally, I cannot warm up to the American girls," interpolated the first mate. "They remind me of dried herrings—skinny, half-dead creatures. All they want is money, money, money."

"Ugh, how can anybody live in such a country?" Mevrouw Vogt-Bensdorp shuddered. "No culture, no traditions, just the almighty dollar and jazzing around the whole time with the cocktails."

"You know, I had an experience," Captain van Popinjay mused. "I was during the war in the same prison camp with some Yank soldiers and you can't even understand what language the *Dummkopfs* are talking."

"No, it's easy," the chief engineer corrected him. He turned to me with a mischievous twinkle. "Coca-Cola hot dog stick 'em up!" The group dissolved in helpless laughter. I disengaged my fingers from the arm of my chair, which I had squeezed to matchwood, loosened my collar to afford more clearance for my Adam's apple, and stood up.

*"Do you know that it is not safe for a girl
to go out on the streets of Chicago?"*

"If you muzzlers have finished sprinkling Paris green on my appetite," I said courteously, "we should like to be excused to disinfect ourselves before dining. Don't bother to get up, gentlemen; my wife isn't used to these little niceties." Descending the companion-way, I overheard them agreeing that all Americans were roughnecks and that our social graces were on a par with those of the African wart-hog.

The meal that followed these didoes was no less enchanting. Prepared with a shrewd eye to the ninety-degree temperatures, it led off with a large basin of boiling pea soup dotted with sausage and booby-trapped with a pig's knuckle sprinkled with fried onions. On the heels of this dainty *Vorspeise* came *paupiettes de veau,* a highly lethal meatball garnished with soggy boiled potatoes and hillocks of that most diuretic of all vegetables, purslane. I cannot honestly say I wolfed the *paupiettes* down greedily, principally because, back in 1932, I fed one of them to a champion schnauzer I was bringing back from Europe on the old S. S. *Columbus* and the poor beast dropped dead off the Hen and Chickens lightship. In the sweet-meat division of the *Kochleffel's* menu, the choice of dessert generally lay between semolina pudding, a tasteless batter that paralyzed the craw on contact, and the epicurean nonesuch called Gouda, whose eso-teric flavor I could never distinguish from mouse cheese. To add a final fillip, our dismal groceries were served at breakneck tempo by seven Chinese waiters and enlivened with further running commentary from the Lowlanders on our children's table manners, slovenly dress, and general swinishness.

Once, however, we managed to anesthetize ourselves to a few minor details like the food and the unrelenting xenophobia, shipboard life fell into a fairly pleasant pattern. There were always enough fresh excitements—flying fish, squalls, prahus, sea birds, and innumerable islands—to punctuate our indolent routine, and it was difficult to believe, the morning we anchored at Tandjong Priok, the harbor of Batavia, that the South China Sea lay behind us. Since the steamer was due to sail the next morning for Surabaya, our glimpse of Batavia was hardly more than fleeting. Through the good offices of a friend of Hirschfeld's— who, incidentally, had traversed this territory fifteen years before and left a trail of worthless chits—we were privileged to drive around the city, glut ourselves with dream-boat Chinese food, and visit the museum. Batavia, apart from the old fort and a sprinkling of seventeenth-century houses, offers approximately as much appeal to the senses as Poughkeepsie, except that it is hotter and devoid of Vassar girls; but the museum is a fit subject for dithyrambs, and were it not for the fact that a dithyrambectomy in childhood inhibits me from using them freely, I could unlimber some pretty lush superlatives. The Hindu-Brahmin sculptures from the Borobudur, the batiks, and the jewelry in the Gold Room certainly dwarf any similar collections in the West; and among other charming relics on view, if the sightseer's arches can stand the gaff, is the very room

Captain Bligh occupied after his epochal longboat voyage from the South Pacific to Timor, containing some exceptional memorabilia. There were in the capital, it should be noted, no visible signs of the bloodletting that was rife in the interior of Java, the daily ambush of Dutch convoys and the extinction of whole kampongs in reprisal. The Dutch, apparently impervious to world-wide censure of their invasion of the Republic of Indonesia, were currently pretending that their *coup de main* was successful and that everyone would be playing patty-cakes shortly. The truth was, nevertheless, that they controlled only a few isolated areas and those only by overwhelming weight of arms. You had merely to witness the sullen contempt with which the Javanese treated their white protectors to realize that the imperial goose was cooked forever— a dismaying fact from which Britain in Malaya and France in Indo-China were still girlishly hiding their eyes.

Soon after the *Kochleffel* cleared Tandjong Priok for Semarang, three new passengers made their appearance: Mr. Chen, a young Chinese businessman en route, like ourselves, to the Moluccas, and a Mr. and Mrs. Hoogmeister. Mr. Chen was one of those fantastic Celestials who, at twenty-four, have acquired the poise and commercial acumen of a merchant prince. He knew to a decimal what the zloty and the pengö were being quoted at in the free markets of Tangier and Bangkok, he had dealt in every outlandish com-

modity from gum copal to rhinoceros horn, and there
was hardly a port from Tsingtao to Thursday Island
he had not set foot in at one time or another. His shy
and self-deprecatory manner concealed a host of ac-
complishments; he played the electric guitar like
Charlie Christians and the violin passably, was an
adept sleight-of-hand performer and a formidable opponent at chess, and had an absolutely hypnotic touch
with cards. The impact of so versatile a talent upon
our children, who by now had had a surfeit of flying
fish, was as pronounced as though Houdini himself
had come on board. Within half an hour, the three
were holed up in our cabin with cigars clenched in
their teeth (my daughter handled hers surprisingly for
a girl of eleven), playing canasta for three guilders a
point. Perhaps our most grisly moment, though, oc-
curred when we stumbled on Abby and Mr. Chen in the
smoking saloon, sawing out a 'cello-and-violin duet of
"Slow Boat to China." The possibility that I had
whelped a future member of Phil Spitalny's all-girl
orchestra so completely unnerved me that I collapsed
in my wife's arms and had to be revived with intra-
venous injections of Courvoisier.

Mr. and Mrs. Hoogmeister, the other new arrivals,
constituted no such social addition but were quite as
remarkable. The former was a wizen-faced, Ichabod
Cranelike exporter from Celebes, married a fortnight to
a Frenchwoman thirty years his junior and uxorious
to the point of folly. Though the lady was not downright misshapen, she was certainly nothing to heat

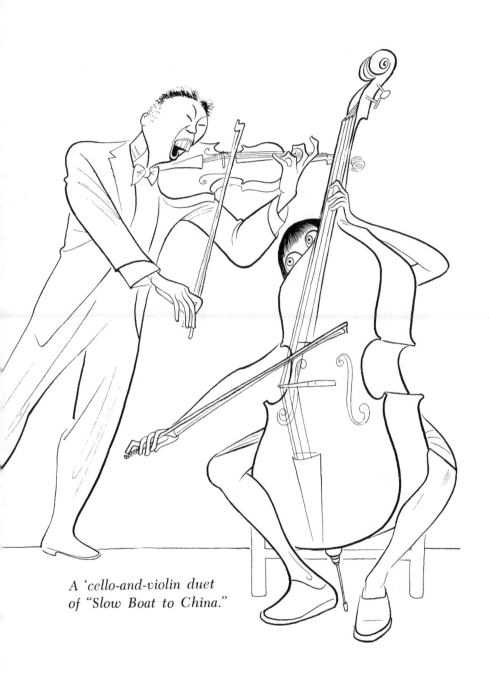

A 'cello-and-violin duet of "Slow Boat to China."

the blood, and the surveillance he kept her under, his elaborate concern lest she stray out of his sight, brought to mind a Palais Royal farce. Madame Hoogmeister was seeing the Orient for the first time, her husband confided to me; he had fixed up what he described as a lavish home for her in Macassar, complete with a new Studebaker and a Frigidaire—had, in fact, gone to the devil's own expense to gratify her caprice, but it was pathetically plain that the bride was already fairly cheesed off on her surroundings. She kept complaining about the heat, the helicopter cockroaches which disrupted her sleep, the coarse and uninspired food. Hoogmeister was in a swivet; one's heart went out to him since he was, by his own admission, such a humane and lovable figure. When he talked about the Indonesians, whom he called "my children," the hackles were assured plenty of exercise. He was fond of observing that in the good old times, the natives always crouched on the floor in his presence to show their subservience, but nowadays, emboldened by our American rubbish about democracy, they invariably stood up, as if they were his equals.

"Mind you, I'm a decent chap," he protested. "If a coolie asked me for a light for his cigarette, in a proper tone, I'd gladly give him one." His wife cocked her head and regarded him affectionately.

"You really like these people, don't you, dear?" she inquired.

"Like them?" he repeated oracularly. "I don't like them—I *love* them!"

Any expectation we entertained of visiting Semarang, we learned on reaching it, was fatuous; the Dutch military had proscribed the port as too dangerous for civilians to land. Consequently, the ship lay well out in the bay while its cargo was being lightered ashore through swarms of sharks and angelfish ceaselessly circling about for food. As landlubbers might, we were understandably impressed by sharks fourteen feet in length, but Captain van Popinjay pooh-poohed them as small fry. In 1928, he informed us, he had captured a thirty-foot specimen off Billiton whose stomach contained an amazing variety of objects. I cannot remember them all, but among them were a complete set of the Waverley novels in half Morocco, a bicycle pump, an ocarina, a roll of sprigged muslin, a miter box, and an early portrait of the Duchess of Richmond by Lely.

It was somewhere between Semarang and Surabaya that I began to get an inkling of the friendly interest being taken in our party by the Dutch. Father de Groot had repeatedly tried to inveigle me into a political discussion, hoping I would reveal myself as a secret agent, but to no avail. One afternoon, the children bounced in with tidings that he had been grilling them about my opinions. Was it not true that their daddy held a Communist party card and deeply admired Russia? Did he seem distressed or jubilant at the news that Dewey had lost the election? For whom had he voted—Wallace? Had they noticed any bearded individuals, redolent of vodka and caraway seeds, frequenting our home? The tots conducted themselves with textbook sang-froid. They replied that on the few occasions I came home, I was too befuddled with malt to talk intelligibly about anything, let alone politics. Having spent most of my life in jail, they continued, I was ineligible to vote. The only bearded visitor they recollected was a man named Hirschfeld, who drew amusing doodles on cardboard but otherwise appeared to have no grasp on reality. Father de Groot retired snarling to his breviary and thereafter made only one reference to any of us. He told Mr. Chen that our children were much too precocious.

On Sunday noon, in a white-hot glare that made the pavements dance and shriveled the brain to a raisin, the four of us teetered down the main street of Surabaya toward its principal oasis, the Oranje Hotel. More leisurely and countrified than Batavia, and perceptibly cleaner, Java's second largest city also seemed far more colorful. The people strolling past represented every conceivable racial strain: pert Javanese youths in immaculate whites and Moslem caps, tall melancholy Hindus, Buginese boatmen, delectable Madurese ladies in bajus and sarongs, and prosperous Chinese compradores, twirling cotton umbrellas, in striped pajamas and sola topi. The particular sound that struck the ear and set the rhythm of Surabaya was the measured, musical clack of teklets, the wooden clogs worn everywhere in the archipelago, but by nobody with as much élan as the Madurese charmers I refer to. Stooping to retrieve one that had fallen squarely in my path (a teklet, that is), I suddenly found myself swept full-tilt into the Oranje lobby by my wife.

The people strolling past
represented every conceivable racial strain.

"I know that gambit, Jack," she said coldly. "You're stalemated before you start. Now you freeze right there while I scare up some *rijsttafel.*" Two hours later, distended with rice, we picked our way heavily to a stifling movie theater where we sat like overfed pythons until sundown. The feature was some hoary masterpiece with Esther Ralston and Monte Blue, but it made no evident difference to the Javanese consumers or the thirty-odd Dutch troopers scattered about the house with carbines on their backs. I was told on returning to the ship that we had seriously imperiled our lives entering the cinema, as some dissident had tossed a grenade into it the previous week. My wife, with her eyes fixed on Father de Groot, commented in offhand fashion that explosives were second nature to me, since I had for years been personal bodyguard to Joseph Stalin. The padre gave her a sour grimace and buried his nose in his semolina.

The night before the *Kochleffel* was due in Macassar was a busy one. In our sweltering stateroom, tripping over each other's feet as we worked, the signora and I laboriously packed our anarchical baggage—unknowing that for the next four days, owing to the shortage of hotel space in Macassar, we would be forced to remain *in situ.* Then, weak with exhaustion, we crawled out on the forward boat-deck to drink in the cool midnight breeze blowing up from the Arafura Sea. A heavy foot-fall sounded near us; dimly in the glow of his cigar stump, I discerned the features of Captain van Popin-jay.

"Well," he remarked, indicating the East Indies with a proprietary wave, "you don't have anything like this in America, do you? Go on—take a good look, it belongs to everybody."

"Check," I agreed, "and when he finally realizes it, sugar, you'd better stay in bed with your hat on."

6

Fifteen Dutch on a Red Man's Chest

Everybody was being excessively kind, and kindest of all was Mr. Smit. There were no limits to Mr. Smit's benevolence; waves of cordiality radiated from him like heat from a diaper-drier as he leaned forward across the rattan table and smoothly expounded to me the complex Indonesian political situation. Outside, in the dismal, sprawling dock area of Macassar, principal port of the island of Celebes, the torrential rain of the west monsoon drummed on the godowns; from time to time, a vicious gust rattled the windows of the ship's lounge, forcing Mr. Smit to inflect more precisely, but his voice never lost its silky, insinuating purr.

"Suicide, sheer suicide," he was saying. "I tell you, my dear chap, on the day these unfortunate natives are allowed to govern themselves, you are going to witness the greatest catastrophe in history. My heart"— he placed a large, plump, strangler's hand on his damp bosom to indicate where that organ lay lurking—"my heart goes out to them." Tears of compassion glistened in his pale Malemute eyes, and as the familiar old glycerin bubbled forth, I began to experience the sense of *déjà vu* which had obsessed me the past fortnight. It was the same litany of persecution we had evoked from every Dutch colonial since entering the archipelago—the black ingratitude of their subjects, the mendacity and guile of the Republican leaders, the intolerable presumption of the United Nations in obtruding itself into a domestic quarrel. It was crystal-clear that if I were ever going to escape from Mr. Smit's hypnotic mumble, I would have to resort to desperate measures. Under pretext of refilling his glass with Bols, I dexterously upset the bottle in his lap and we both sprang up, our foreheads colliding violently in midair.

"Look here, I'm most frightfully sorry," I apologized, retrieving the bottle and inadvertently spilling half of it on his shirt. "Let me get you a little ketchup or something to sprinkle on that before it stains."

"No, no, thank you," Mr. Smit protested, backing away. "It's nothing at all—I was going anyway——"

"Nonsense!" I interrupted. "Here's some soy-bean sauce on the sideboard—no, Worcestershire's better ——" Holding on to his jacket and using his wrist as a lever, I wrestled him unobtrusively toward the accommodation ladder. As he backed down it, agitatedly assuring me that he would return to complete my political orientation, my wife and bairns sprinted across the quay from the customs barrier. Soaked to the skin, tingling with irritation and heat rash, they clawed their way up the ladder and inevitably became entangled with Mr. Smit. By the time the Laocoön group unscrambled itself and my family gained the deck, the mem was buzzing like a wasp.

"Who was that confounded idiot?" she sputtered, her magnificent bosom heaving in accordance with the laws governing the upheaval of magnificent bosoms.

"Oh, just another exposed nerve," I replied carelessly. "He controls all the copra in this bailiwick. He'd like to know just what we're doing out here."

"So would I," she said vengefully. "Listen, I've been in some pretty abysmal drops since I threw in my lot with yours, but of all the backward, stultified flea-bags on earth——"

"Steady on, Cassandra," I soothed her. "The *Cinnabar* tied up an hour ago; we weigh tomorrow on the tide." The news that our exile in Macassar was ended produced the reaction I had anticipated. For the previous

For the previous four days we had been
vegetating at the dockside of Macassar.

four days, we had been vegetating aboard the *Koch-leffel* at the dockside, awaiting the small coasting steamer that would carry us into the Moluccas. The distractions of Macassar at any time, and particularly during the rainy season, are hardly such as to earn it the reputation of a spa. True, there is a famous old harbor where, by scaling a barbed-wire fence, you may catch a glimpse of some quaint native prahus, and for lovers of sixteenth-century Portuguese forts, there is a passable sixteenth-century Portuguese fort; but the town, a huddle of bleak and pungent alleys, does not twine itself around the heart and the population seemed merely an Asiatic version of a West Virginia mining community. As for the Dutch contingent, a cross-section of which we reveled with at a social club called the Harmonie, it was less than the gayest society in memory. Most of the men bore a chilling resemblance to either Baldur von Schirach or Himmler; their ladies, with minor exceptions, were cumbrous, hostile, and notably devoid of chic. Possibly it was the music, a series of Wiener waltzes danced with exuberance and no grace whatever, that gave the occasion a highly Germanic flavor, but Milady and I were forced, at the conclusion of the evening, to confess without prejudice that it had been one of the more loathsome of our lives.

It would be cheeky to suppose that our brief stay in Macassar enriched the folklore of that dingy outpost, and yet I think that nobody who was privileged to watch our removal from the *Kochleffel* to the *Cinnabar*

will ever forget it. In the estimation of several waterfront loungers (whose opinion is always authoritative),
it was the single greatest achievement since the con-
struction of the Assouan Dam, the restoration of Ang-
kor Wat, and the diversion of the Yellow River. When
our trunks, satchels, hatboxes, duffel bags, baskets,
portmanteaux, and parcels were finally piled on the
deck of the *Cinnabar* by nine panting coolies, they
formed a cone visible ten miles at sea. Predictions of
disaster, naturally, flew thick and fast; it was pointed
out that the ship had developed a dangerous list to
port and Captain Versteegh, her master, gloomily
prophesied that we would founder in the first blow,
but fortunately for all concerned, most of our kit top-
pled over the side as soon as we got under way.

Whether the vessel would have caused a naval archi-
tect to throw his cap into the air is debatable; to my
layman's eye, she appeared a marvel of compactness,
comfort, and stability. Though displacing only two
thousand tons, she carried four hundred passengers
(the majority of them in deck class), thirty cows, three
hundred chickens, a dozen pigs, and an impressive
quantity of mixed cargo ranging from tractors to cold
storage eggs. She was, in point of fact, an engaging
combination of Toonerville Trolley and Noah's Ark,
delivering mail, freight, and contract labor to the farther
reaches of East Indonesia and gathering copra in return, and as a vehicle from which to observe some of
the most breath-taking scenery in the Orient, she was
unsurpassed.

The loveliness of the islands and the sense of enchantment with which they instill the traveler have been captured with such fidelity by Conrad, Maugham, and Tomlinson—as well as by Alfred Russel Wallace in his superb and ageless *The Malay Archipelago*—that any lesser artisan who tries to emulate them may well wind up gelding the lily. In my own case, I can testify that as the *Cinnabar* moved up the western rim of Celebes, tarrying briefly at obscure outposts like Pare-Pare, Donggala, Ternate, and Batjan, I was caught up in a mood of rapture and euphoria so intense that my family became actively concerned. I began rising at dawn, declaiming fragments of Pierre Loti to the setting sun, and studying astronomy; made plans to sever all ties with civilization, install myself on a coral reef, and rove the South Seas in an auxiliary yawl; and altogether comported myself in an exalted, swashbuckling fashion reminiscent of the senior Fairbanks or a schoolboy in love. The fever reached a crescendo one afternoon at Ternate as we stood on the tumbledown escarpment of an old Dutch fortification, giant coconut palms nodding gently about us and breakers pounding on the black volcanic beach below.

"Well, shipmates," I said, encompassing the scene with a dramatic, sweeping gesture, "it's been a long, weary search, but I've found it at last."

"Found what?" my wife glowered, disengaging a leech from her instep.

"The land of heart's desire," I said quietly, my noble profile silhouetted against the horizon like Robinson

The fever reached a crescendo
one afternoon at Ternate.

Jeffers. "A safe anchorage from the storms and petty distractions of life. A snug eyrie where, as the sea birds sport ceaselessly overhead and the majestic diapason of the Pacific echoes in my ear, I can achieve that inner harmony to which Lao-tzu and Gautama Buddha point the way. Now the first thing we need," I said briskly, casting a shrewd, experienced glance about me, "is a rude shelter of some sort." Suiting the deed to the word, I extracted a gold penknife and started to hack down one of the palms. What was my chagrin, on turning a second later, to find that my kinsmen had taken a powder and were climbing back into our rented jeep.

"We're just nipping back to New York for a few supplies," my wife explained apologetically. "You know, corn meal and linsey-woolsey and stuff. You stay right here; we won't be a minute." Obviously I could not permit a woman and two small tots to drive unescorted through five miles of jungle terrain, and since the blade of my knife had snapped off in any case, partially sundering an artery in my wrist, I decided to accompany them back to the ship. My vigilance proved extremely far-sighted, for I discovered subsequently that there was not a granule of marinated herring on Ternate, and had we settled there, we might have been exposed to untold hardships.

After the bile displayed by so many of the Dutch theretofore, Captain Versteegh's amiability and desire to please came as a heartening change; throughout the twenty-three-day voyage, he exhibited a solicitude

97

for our welfare and a zeal in organizing tours, picnics, and similar diversions that made him an anomaly among his countrymen. Under his guidance, we saw much we would otherwise have missed—the villages of the Minahassa, the residences of the sultans of Ternate and Batjan, the sinister lake straight out of Edgar Allan Poe named Tanah Tinggalam which had swallowed up three native compounds when it was created by an earthquake, and the stupefying flora and fauna, the cockatoos, apes, and orchids, which flourish in those incredible islands. One of the more bizarre spectacles was a collection of two hundred Flying Fortresses and several thousand jeeps crumbling away in the bush at Morotai, the huge air base of the last war. This edifying sight, it should be noted, was shown us as an example of Yankee prodigality and waste; our cicerone, a Dutch subaltern, underscored it with footnotes on our dollar diplomacy and pharisaism distilled of purest snake venom. It was really quite awe-inspiring, as the trip progressed, to discover with what revulsion the United States was regarded by the Dutch in Indonesia. America, we found, occupied the curious dual role of skinflint and sucker, the usurer bent on exacting his pound of flesh and the hapless pigeon whose poke was a challenge to any smart grifter. The aversion assumed a thousand exotic shapes; whenever conversation flagged, some body-snatcher could always be depended on to conjecture when the next depression would engulf America or the atomic bomb obliterate New York. The most studied insult I heard of was directed at a young American missionary who journeyed with us from Ternate to Amboina. He was chatting one evening with a couple of Batjan planters and their wives when the subject of Hawaii's impending recognition as our forty-ninth state arose. One of the planters suddenly slapped his knee.

"That reminds me," he said, turning to his wife. "Did you tell the houseboy?"

"Tell him what?" she asked.

"Why, to sew another star on that American flag we use for a dishrag," he said with a feline grin. "After all, we can't lag behind the times, can we, gentlemen?"

"Remind me to sew another star on that American flag," he said with a feline grin.

Our missionary friend was in something of a dilemma. His natural impulse to hang a mouse on the speaker's eye clashed with his clerical vows, and he felt moreover that his usefulness would be restricted in the cooler where the Dutch would most certainly have flung him. He therefore excused himself with a tortured smile and retired to his stateroom to reread certain admonitions on turning the other cheek—as striking an instance of Christian self-restraint as any in the revealed writings.

The gleam of the stiletto was nowhere as pronounced, perhaps, as at Sorong, the western tip of New Guinea, where we ran full tilt into the prettiest little case of industrial despotism imaginable. An oil company town complete with electrified fences, searchlights, armed guards, and all the standard appurtenances of the detention camp, Sorong will never dispute with Bar Harbor as the vacationist's choice, but it was the only contact we were having with New Guinea and I had hoped to see at least a bit of its fabulous jungle at first hand. The anchor chains had barely stopped quivering before I was disabused. An insufferably pompous, pear-shaped young Hollander boarded the *Cinnabar*, introduced himself as Van Wuppertal, public relations officer of the firm, and demanded my credentials. I presented my parole card from the Lewisburg Penitentiary, together with a certificate to the effect that I had been cured of mopery and drug addiction, and having scanned them minutely, he handed down a mandate from the front office. The management, he announced, had graciously consented to our landing at Sorong the following day for a period of two hours, when we would be taken on a tour of the oil installations.

"Please forgive me for sounding blasé," I returned, "but in the eleven years I spent in Southern California, I became reasonably browned off on high octane. My family and I would like to take a gander at the greenery. Capricious though it sounds, we ache to see a bird of paradise on the wing."

"The whim of the foreign journalist is not law in Sorong," retorted Van Wuppertal. "This is private territory, and you will be shown that portion of it we deem fit. Good morning." The notion that an oil concern had superseded the Dutch crown and was administering New Guinea was so captivating that I rounded up Captain Versteegh (who, of course, promptly blew a gasket), and we called on the assistant resident for a clarification of Sorong's status. This diplomat, lodged on an atoll offshore bearing the apposite name of the Island of Doom, also flew into a passion. New Guinea was ours to come and go as we pleased, he thundered; heads would roll in the sand if any man moved to gainsay us. He urged us to proceed on the double into Sorong, he would show those beggars who was master here, but at the same time, he disavowed any responsibility for our safety. In short, he gave a splendid imitation of a man badly frightened by an oil well.

The next morning, accordingly, the four of us, chaperoned by the captain in his snowiest drill, piled into

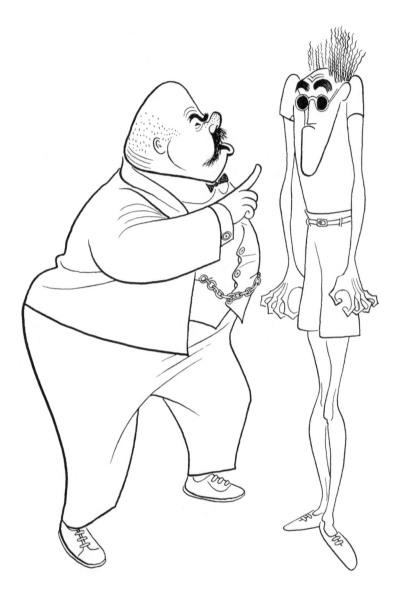

"The whim of the foreign journalist is not law in Sorong,"
retorted Van Wuppertal.

the latter's gig and made for the mainland. Van Wuppertal must have been observing our sortie through a spyglass, because he was waiting on the jetty in a state of considerable perturbation. Apparently our intransigence had created a situation.

"E-excuse me, ladies and gentlemen," he puffed, "but this is all highly irregular. Where are you going?"

"To the jungle, Mac," spoke up my first-born, squaring his jaw, "and we don't want any of your chicken-fat, savvy?" Checking a violent impulse to kick a small boy in the sweetbreads, Van Wuppertal feverishly bade the rest of the party wait and rushed me to his superior's office. The company's Number Two man was a museum specimen, a knifelike Junker whose quartz eyes and pitiless mouth would have endeared him to the *Herrenvolk.* In a tone that beautifully blended contempt with condescension, he made it evident that he ranked my profession between that of an iguana and a poor-box thief. The company, he snapped, had suffered some slight annoyance at the hands of an Australian pen-pusher who had published damaging reports about labor conditions in Sorong. He wanted it understood that his personnel was supremely content with its lot, and, he added significantly, he hoped I was not one of these snoopers and troublemakers. I assured him that next to the Magna Carta, I worshiped the stockholder's dividend more than life itself; no muckraker I, but a vapid little tomtit writing elegiacs about temple bells and lepidoptera. Thanks to my beguiling bourgeois aspect and the fact that I was accompanied by my family, his suspicions were allayed, and in Van Wuppertal's custody, we were permitted to venture fifteen kilometers into the forest.

Presumably the birds of paradise, the Papuans, and the giant butterflies had also been warned of our advent and had stampeded, for all we saw in the end was impenetrable timber, a gravel road flanked by a pipeline, and a series of roadblocks at which our identities were methodically rechecked. The coup de grâce, though, awaited us on our return to the jetty. We were about to leave Sorong to her rosy future of development by the termite and Dutch capital when Van Wuppertal drew me aside.

"There is just one more detail," he said. "Before you publish anything on what you have seen here, you will first submit a copy to the company for approval."

"Would you mind repeating that rather more slowly?" I asked, cupping my ear. "I have a feeling that you have just said something quite epochal."

"Certainly," he answered. "You must show us whatever you write before it is printed. So we can judge whether it is suitable for public consumption."

"You wouldn't be trying to tamper with Mummy's prose by any chance, would you?" I inquired. "You know, we have a nasty name for that sort of thing in the States."

"I am not interested in the States," said Van Wuppertal loftily. "We are in New Guinea at the moment."

"That we are, Peaches," I agreed, "and I'll tell you what you can do with it." I told him, and when I had finished, I left New Guinea. If he is still standing there as I last saw him, they'll never need a lighthouse in Sorong.

A hundred and twenty miles southeast of Amboina in the vast and lonely tropical sea lies a microscopic cluster of islands known as the Banda group. From them, in 1604, stemmed the rich spice trade which became the cornerstone of Dutch imperial power; even today, the reputation of their nutmeg and mace is unrivaled among gourmets and those exacting folk who pride themselves on their condiments. As the political importance of spice and the Netherlands declined across the centuries, however, the Banda group was forgotten; and since they are almost entirely inaccessible, offer no facilities to the wayfarer, are reputed to be malarial, and contain a population of minor anthropological interest, their appeal nowadays is fairly negligible. Why, consequently, I should have bamboozled myself into visiting them, at the price of abandoning my family and pitting myself against one of the world's most treacherous oceans in an antiquated, greasy launch manned by a bunch of untrained Indonesian sailors, was something of a conundrum. Exactly who did I think I was anyway, Captain Joshua Slocum? And what kind of insane romantic compulsion possessed a sedentary, diffident taxpayer of forty-five to suddenly start behaving like Vasco da Gama? These and a host of equally wintry reflections surged through my mind as I stood on the stringpiece at Amboina in the gathering dusk and watched the *Cinnabar* back slowly into midstream. The faces of my wife and children began growing indistinct; in a few moments, the handkerchiefs they waved were no longer discernible against the blurred bulk of the ship. The native boy assigned to conduct me aboard the *Sembilan* touched my arm respectfully. I handed down my gear into his dinghy, scrambled after him, and we rocked away toward the buoy where the launch lay moored.

"*Tuan mengerti Inggris?*" I asked him in my execrable Berlitz Malay, which was to say, Do you understand English, Jack?

"*Tidak, Tuan,*" he replied, shaking his head in the negative.

"Good," I said, relieved. "Because then I can make a promise without any fear you'll hold me to it. If I ever so much as budge off the island of Manhattan, I want you to take an outsize baseball bat . . ." I gave him quite a lengthy set of instructions before I was through, and I do hope he was telling me the truth. I'd hate to think I had misplaced my confidence.

7

Refrain, Audacious Tar

T HE CABIN was roughly eight feet square, just high enough for a malnourished orangutan to stand upright in, and unspeakably hot. Down through its doll's-size hatchway billowed wave on wave of Diesel exhaust as the cutter *Sembilan*, three hours out of Amboina for the Banda Islands, labored in the long, rolling swell. Eyeballs awash in their sockets, perspiration spouting from my every pore, I lay spread-eagled in one of the two squalid bunks, listening to my heartbeat accelerate and retard in rhythm with the engines beyond the bulkhead. Apart from an inconsequential neuralgic headache, a vague queasiness in the tripes, and the specious sensation of claustrophobia familiar to anyone who has ever been buried alive, I felt like a million dollars.

Recumbent on my roach-ridden pallet and sucking deep draughts of monoxide into my lungs, I congratulated myself thrice over. Without an inborn flair for entangling myself in lunatic enterprises, a positive genius for coaxing chaos out of thin air, I too might at this very moment be caught in the same tragic imbroglio as my family. I envisioned them aboard the *Cinnabar* where I had left them, with nothing to assuage their thirst but tall, beaded glasses of lemonade and Dutch export beer, reduced to eating *rijsttafel*, fresh pineapple, crispy noodles, egg roll, little prawns, and similar starvation fare. What could such earthlings know of the savage exultation of subduing the elements, the sense of accomplishment that springs from lying half dead in a greasy bunk adrift on an alien sea? Ah, but they would pay handsomely for their prudence, I promised myself, grinding my teeth. I thought of the endless boring yarns I would spin around our fireside on future winter nights; in my mind's eye, I rehearsed the lurid catalogue of typhoon, shipwreck, shark, and piracy I would distill from my dash to Banda Neira. Just as I was whipping myself into a meringue of indignation—for obviously my kin could have prevented me from this undertaking had they cared a hoot for my safety—a pair of pajama-clad legs

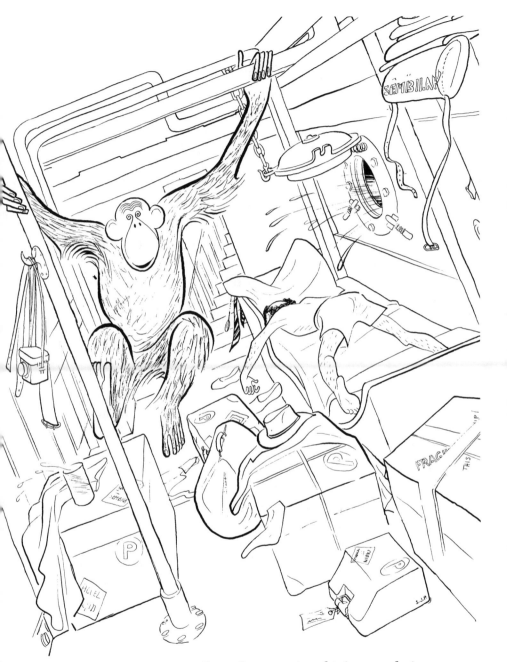

The cabin was just high enough for a malnourished orangutan to stand upright in.

materialized in the hatchway and the master of the *Sembilan* vaulted down. A taciturn, arid martinet who taught seamanship at the naval training school in Amboina, Onderdonk was the perfect movie stereotype of the German U-boat commander. His gimlet eyes, rat-trap mouth, and visored cap could only have been conceived by Central Casting.

"Why are you hiding down here?" he demanded sharply. "I arranged for us to sleep on top of the wheelhouse." Brushing aside my whimpered protest that I adored the smell of bilge, he jerked the pillow from under my head and dragged me summarily up on deck. My arrival there apparently unchained the full malevolence of the Banda Sea; at once the *Sembilan* executed a succession of sinuous bumps like Georgia Sothern and dropped forward into illimitable space. The story of my climb up the wheelhouse in the blackness, drenched with spray and clinging to nailheads and rivets, is a saga still recounted in whispers wherever alpinists forgather. It was a nerve-racking ordeal, but child's play compared to what lay in wait. Two rickety canvas cots stood side by side in an area barely twice their size; around the edge of the roof, sole guarantee against our being swept overboard, ran a flimsy handrail of iron pipe. Had the cots been stationary, they would have presented no problem, but with each wave, the centrifugal roll of the cutter caused them to slither outward and dangle perilously over the drink. I finally managed to capture one, an operation comparable to bulldogging a steer or wrapping a live herring in newspaper, and stretching out six feet of sinewy oleomargarine, composed my thoughts for sleep.

There are certain interludes in one's life from which the memory recoils; the next six hours of mine were writ on water in every sense of the word. I passed them woven around the handrail in the manner of a morning-glory, one elbow and knee locked to it for protection and the rest of me jouncing loosely on the cot. Four or five times, under the impact of an especially heavy sea, the cot slid away altogether and I was left revolving on my perch like a broiler in a Sixth Avenue rotisserie. It is not an attitude conducive to sustained thought, but I succeeded in covering an astonishing amount of ground; I postulated and solved a dozen domestic and international crises, struck several codicils from my will, and composed a sheaf of stinging, witty letters to persons who had given me umbrage. Luckily I was on the *qui vive* and primed to take over command, for Onderdonk, sunk in a brutish slumber, seemed lost to any shred of responsibility. Once, in fact, I did issue an order to abandon ship when we were reeling under several mountainous combers, but the sailors, a cowardly lot, pretended my voice was inaudible above the tempest and hid in the washroom. Realizing the jig was up unless I acted with celerity, I threw my weight to the opposite side of the vessel; there was a moment of suspense while all hearts beat high; then, timbers groaning, the *Sembilan* slowly righted herself and continued on her course. Whether or not my quick thinking was solely instrumental in

111

I was left revolving like a
broiler in a Sixth Avenue rotisserie.

averting disaster, modesty forbids me to say, but it had certainly been a narrow squeak.

Somehow, by that mysterious process of erosion which operates even during moments of deepest travail, the night wore away at last. The hands began stirring about and coiling rope for us to trip over, the cook brewed up a species of coffee compounded of acorns and paint remover, and Onderdonk and I, with the assistance of three bottles of Bols, settled down to pass the fifteen hours that remained of the journey. He was, on the whole, one of the least diverting people it has ever been my lot to encounter; despite a lifetime of voyaging around the world, his dialogue was made up entirely of philippics on the laziness and chicanery of the Oriental and recriminations about his ill-fortune. By midafternoon, spleen and Bols exhausted, we sat pickled in melancholy, swaying to the perpetual rise and fall of the brine. The steep volcanic cone of Banda far off on the horizon grew more distinct, but at our snail's pace of six knots and bucking a head wind, it might as easily have been the Jungfrau. It was midnight before the cutter reached the narrow inlet leading into the harbor. Beyond a few scattered natives fishing by torchlight, there was no sign of port, village, or any human habitation. After a vast amount of jockeying and hullabaloo, we made fast to a wharf under the apathetic scrutiny of a score of urchins and pariah dogs. Considering that the Sembilan was the first boat from the outside world in six weeks, popular excitement could scarcely be said to be running at fever pitch.

113

"I—er—I don't suppose there's a Statler in town, is there, friend?" I asked, approaching one of the dogs who seemed less mangy than his fellows. "I'm a stranger here and I wondered where I could latch on to a nice steak." Onderdonk must have assumed that I was trying to glean some political information, because he bustled up officiously before the animal could return a civil answer and ordered me to follow him. We stumbled through a cluster of weedy streets lined with bombed-out dwellings and arrived in due course at an awesome structure resembling a Southern antebellum mansion. This, I was to discover, was one of thirty equally splendid houses built by the Dutch perkeniers, or nutmeg planters, when Banda was at her crest. To convey the magnificence of these establishments without lapsing into the florid style of Ouida or Edgar Saltus is not easy. They all had lofty Corinthian porticoes, reception halls and bedchambers without end, floors of eighteenth-century tile and Carrara marble, servants' quarters, and formal gardens; but more remarkable, the majority were available at a ceiling rent of a dollar and fifty cents a month. If the foregoing sounds overly idyllic to anyone caught in a housing shortage, it is well to remember that every rose has its thorn. Banda, no matter what part of the world you live in, is approximately thirteen thousand miles away and a very tough commute.

The scatter to which Onderdonk had conducted me, it turned out, was the residence of the *controleur*, the official representing Dutch authority thereabouts. He

"I—er—I don't suppose there's a Statler in town, is there, friend?"

proved to be a small, rabbity Eurasian in fire-sale pajamas, who inexplicably decided we had come to check up on his administration and began gibbering with terror. On being assured that we merely wished a shakedown for the night, he recovered a measure of calm and installed us in the government resthouse. I daresay the venerable four-poster bed I occupied was worth its weight in auctioneers' huzzas, but viewed primarily as a kip, it was pretty spotty. As I threshed around on its rope springs, inhaling the dust of a mosquito bar that had not been laundered since the accession of William III, I was ready to trade all Tartary for a standard box mattress. Our rest was also punctuated by an intermittent bombardment of nuts from the great kenari trees overhead, which smote the corrugated iron roof until it echoed. All in all, Onderdonk was in a fairly vixenish mood over the morning tea (I, needless to say, was an angel), and I was cheered when the tension fast developing between us was relieved by the sudden appearance of Axel Sundstrom.

Sundstrom was a huge, jovial young Swede who had been sequestered on Banda the three months previous making a documentary film; he had been represented to me in Amboina as an eccentric, but as nearly as I could tell, his only vagary was that he was both amiable and literate, in distinction to my informants. A serious ethnographer and linguist, Sundstrom was no Vine Street Rossellini full of pretension and pat phrases. He had left Stockholm three years before to record the language and customs of some of the lesser-known peoples of Asia; thus far he had photographed the Kali sect in India and the Toradjas of South Celebes, and when his current project was completed, planned to work in Tasmania. He was, of course, his own cameraman, cutter, and technical crew, operating under difficulties few Europeans would care to endure. In Celebes, for example, he had contracted diphtheria, nobody having warned him that the disease was endemic among the Toradjas and that he must be inoculated. It was six days' journey to the nearest hospital in Macassar; the tribesmen, certain he was doomed in any case, refused to transport him there, regarding it as a frivolous waste of manpower. How he cozened them into doing so, in exchange for his tape recorder, and his subsequent trek through the mountains and eleven-week convalescence, made an extraordinary narrative. Yet he was in no way portentous and given to self-dramatization; he related it all with great good-humor as he sat with feet cocked up on a table, a flower behind one ear and his fingers strumming the guitar which seemed to be an essential part of his kit. I suppose what fetched me particularly was his gusto, the contrast between his lively, cultivated curiosity and the sour and sterile provincialism of Onderdonk scowling into his everlasting Bols.

There are unquestionably those who would not be unduly oppressed by Banda's crumbling façades, its gardens choked with tropical undergrowth, and the lackluster, underfed natives wandering in its silent streets. Unfortunately, I am neither lyric poet nor social worker; my temperament does not thrive on the spectacle of vanished grandeur, and by the time we had made a circuit of the marketplace and clambered through Fort Belgica, I was content to step back into my own century. The inclination was strengthened by a visit to Lonthoir, across the bay, where we saw vestiges of the island's once-flourishing nutmeg culture. While interesting from the botanical angle, the plantations seemed less significant than the people who tilled them. By and large, they were as seedy and necessitous a group as I had seen in the archipelago. They were subsisting on a thoroughly vitamin-free diet of grated white sweet potato and sago, they were overrun with malaria, trachoma, rickets, and yaws, and their only educational facility was a primary Islamic school. It was a rather chastening reflection that the spot I stood on was the cradle of the great Dutch commonwealth, that these sickly, defeated people and the deserted mansions across the bay were the end product of three hundred years of empire. If this was the tally of the white man's civilizing influence, it was hardly bizarre that somebody should be asking for a new shuffle.

Thirty-six hours later in Amboina, I sat in the living room of an affluent Cantonese merchant, toying with duck stewed in ginger and listening to his nine-year-old daughter sing that traditional old Chinese ballad, "Always in My Heart." My stomach was still fluttering from the effects of the return voyage of the *Sembilan*, and the young party's reedy soprano was doing nothing to stabilize it. My one consolation lay in the fact that I was not the only victim of a doting papa; a covey of Dutch oil technicians and their wives, passing through on their way from New Guinea to Sydney, had also been dragooned into attending. It was impossible to learn from their bleak and frozen faces which galled them more, the proximity of an American or the child's keening, but they radiated the warmth of a clump of stalagmites. When the gifted entertainer, flushed with her success, began pounding out "Chopsticks" on the piano, I decided the end of the tether had been reached. If there were any obligation to undergo this type of purgatory, I might as well do so at the hands of my own children, whom I was winging to rejoin on Bali the next day; so, bestowing a priceless star sapphire on my host in token of my gratitude—I generally keep a pocketful in my overalls for such eventualities— and sprinkling a little ground glass into the other guests' drinks, I made for the sack.

The flight to Macassar the following afternoon could not have been more uneventful; my fellow passengers, except for gaudier pigmentation and better manners, were as prosy as any you might meet in a New Haven club car. I had checked into the airline hotel, finished dinner, and was undertipping the waiter when adventure suddenly plucked at my lapel. A dusky gentleman in tropical whites, with the face of a weatherbeaten fox, bade me good evening and asked how my sugar

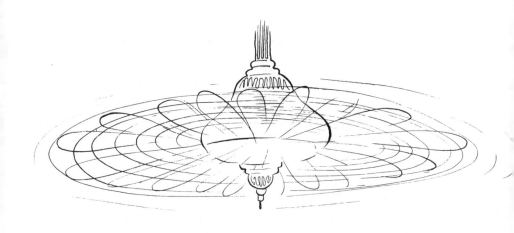

The weirdest business partnership since the South Sea bubble.

refinery in Surabaya was faring. Curious to see what his pitch was, I offered to broach a keg of nails and we adjourned to the bar. In forty-five minutes our acquaintanceship had ripened into the most astonishing business partnership since the South Sea Bubble. It appeared that with my money and Mr. Da Costa's extensive marine experience, we were going to outfit a lugger to dredge for pearl shell and trepang off the Aru Islands. The rewards, and my new-found friend warned me that he was a man who preferred to take the pessimistic view, would be staggering, astronomical. Was I aware what trepang—the bêche-de-mer or sea-cucumber considered a delicacy by the Chinese—was bringing these days?

"Why, they use it instead of gold on the China coast!" Da Costa swore, spitting all over me in his enthusiasm. "And pearl shell, that's what the world is crying for! Think of the uses—souvenir ashtrays, picture frames, paper cutters, buttons! Do you realize how many buttons there are on the average pair of underdrawers?" I began counting the buttons on my underdrawers, but he struck my hand away brusquely. "We haven't time for that now," he rapped. "I tell you, we're in clover—our fortunes are made!"

"What—uh—what sort of a lugger do you see?" I asked, stroking my chin thoughtfully. "Grimsby trawler or more of a flat type?"

"Now you're talking!" approved Da Costa. "That's what I like, a man of action. Let's work up a sketch." After interminable discussion, we evolved a good seaworthy vessel of some three hundred tons with automatic winches and a copper-sheathed hull. My associate was a trifle dubious about the cost of the hull, but when I pointed out the danger of shallow coral reefs, he yielded instanter. "By God," he said admiringly. "I never would have thought of that. You know these waters like a book."

"I've knocked about a bit," I admitted, shifting my quid and my wallet. "There's many an octopus between Merauke and Port Moresby who's sorry he ever crossed tentacles with Errol Flynn." It took nearly two hours and another bottle of Scotch to settle the question of diving dress and crew (I insisted on at least two Kanakas and a swarthy Lascar), and plans complete, we shook hands on the bargain. Da Costa was to depart immediately for a shipyard on eastern Ceram to lay the keel, while I would hasten to Wall Street to float the necessary capital.

"You don't think you could let me have about five American dollars, do you?" he inquired hopefully. "You know, for office expenses, incorporation papers, sealing wax, and so." I explained that a sharp decline in Sumatra pepper had frozen my assets for the nonce, but promised to cable the money as soon as the situation improved in Mincing Lane. Our leave-taking was highly emotional. Da Costa gave way to a sobbing fit and I fell down three times getting back to my room; nevertheless, each of us switched off his light with the conviction that he had put over a pretty shrewd transaction, and I still think I got the better of it.

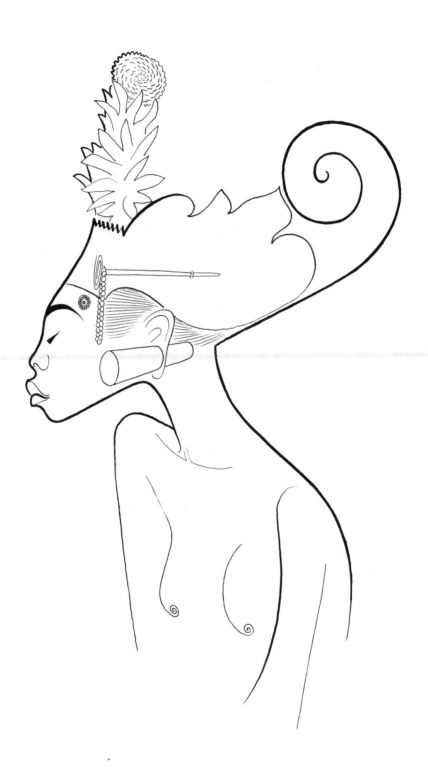

At noon the next day the Dakota that had borne me across the Flores Sea taxied up the runway of the Denpasar airport at South Bali and cut its engines. The heat of midday hung over the trim little airport; in a disembodied, slumbrous haze composed of equal parts of hangover, fatigue, and relief at my deliverance, I was wafted through miles of terraced rice sawahs to luxuries I no longer believed existed, a spotless hotel room and tiled showers. Everything I saw was bathed in the first rosy flush of enchantment—the graceful, smiling Balinese, the shops crammed with carvings and textiles, the stir and bustle of the town. It did not matter that disillusion was inevitable, that I would soon discover the carvings had come from Jersey City and the smiles from contact with tourists. In the glorious here and now, two facts were salient and irrefutable—Onderdonk was fifteen hundred miles to the east and tonight I would sleep on a bed instead of a spit. And brother, that's bliss enough for any boy.

Balinese pastiche

8

Whenas in Sulks My Julia Goes

H AVE YOU EVER BEEN lonely/ Have you ever been blue?" The lachrymose, velveteen voice of Perry Como, released from wax by the dubious magic of a gramophone needle, soared upward on the tropical night, floated across the courtyard of the Princess Hotel in Bali, and wove like a dental drill into the room where I sat sunk in a bamboo armchair. For the fifteenth time in as many minutes, I beat a clenched fist against my skull to relieve the pressure slowly forcing it asunder and strove to focus on the page before me. Lytton Strachey had never been more lucid; his sonorous, balanced sentences, almost Biblical in their majesty, rolled on relentlessly detailing the final tragedy of Chinese Gordon, but concentrate as I might, nothing emerged but the plaintive bleat of unrequited love. Without raising her head from the dressing-table where she was seated lacquering her nails, my wife addressed me.

"Well, Bright Eyes," she remarked in the detached, overcasual manner with which wives introduce a topic they have been brooding over for hours, "if you've finished your imitation of Cozy Cole, I'd like to file a few words. We've been on this island paradise exactly two weeks. When, if I may borrow a phrase from that twilit world of the St. Nicholas Arena and the Hotel Alamac in which you love to skulk, do you propose to throw in the towel?"

Ordinarily, so bumptious a statement would have stung me to a quick retort; I would have annihilated the woman with a single glance, excoriated her for a virago and a Philistine insensitive to the beauty about us, and made her grovel for her presumption. Yet, as I proceeded to take rapid inventory of the past fortnight, there was no denying our sojourn on Bali had been a notably dismal one. Aside from several extraordinary Legong and monkey dances and some really bewitching scenery, the balance definitely stood on the debit side. For nearly the entire period, our young had been hors de combat with dysentery, jungle boils, and ulcers of the leg—none of them especially fatal complaints, to be sure, but frustrating when one's medical kit consisted of phenobarbital and bobbie pins. Through five days of fever and delirium, I myself had wrestled with an unclassified bacillus, now bivouacked in my Eustachian tubes as snugly as a bear in a hollow tree. As for our quarters, which had stirred me to madrigals after the rigors of Banda, they too seemed a little less overwhelming; the arcades lined with machine-made carvings, the fruit salad and dinner music both drawn from cans, and the excessively genteel management, one rapacious eye riveted on the guest's pocketbook, somehow brought to mind a high-class Southern California motel. Granted that the Balinese were engaging, handsome folk and that despite the inroads of tourism, they still retained some of the artistic talent and exotic innocence of their forefathers. The chilling truth, however, was that when you had seen one cremation, one tooth-filing ceremony, and one cockfight, you had seen them all. Lodged in our trunks were the tiger masks, the wayang dolls, the batiks, the krisses, and all the authentic kickshaws that would prove to our detractors that we had actually passed through Bali. There was no point in fighting our custard, in blinking the unblinkable. It was time to vamoose.

Every family has its moments of disrepair, when the collective nose tends to run and the corporate eye to blear, but on the evening mine straggled off the plane in Batavia after eight weeks in the hinterlands of Indonesia, we were a fearsome sight. Fricasseed by the sun, yellowed by quinine, dehydrated to shadows, bellies bloated with the heavy Dutch provender we had been subsisting on, we looked like a provincial company of *Tobacco Road*. Our togs were even more eccentric; the sultana had long since struck her colors and was garbed in palmetto fronds, and the moppets and I were as bankrupt of oomph as Bozo Snyder. All that was lacking to bring us up to concert pitch was six hours of insomnia in a stifling bed and a washbowl stuffed with banana skins, and Destiny had already prepared them. For good measure, she also threw in a wild-animal dealer in the adjoining room, who, as nearly as we could gauge, kept chasing and beating a cassowary all night long. By the time the four of us swayed out of the waiting room of the airport next morning to continue the trip to Singapore and Bangkok, we were so snowbound with seconal that we had to be hoisted into the aircraft. It was just as well I had cushioned my nervous system with the handy white shock absorbers, in view of the cable awaiting us at Singapore. It had been sent by my pettifogging lawyer in New York (collect, of course), and its message was stark and unadorned: "Tenant of your apartment evicted today after gun battle stop Sashes and doors still intact but oh boy stop Have fun cousin you'll need it."

"The spoons!" screamed my wife in a tone that must have penetrated to the headwaters of the Irrawaddy. "I told you not to leave that momzer our silver when we sublet the flat!"

"I didn't leave it!" I shouted. "I locked it in the guest closet!"

"Yes, and gave him a duplicate key," she wailed. "Well, that concludes twenty years of light housekeeping. Easy come, easy go!" The children, not quite comprehending what was afoot but intuitively sensing disaster, burst into convulsive sobs; the other occupants of the plane sprang to the conclusion that I was a wife-beater and began to mutter menacingly; the lingering pain in my throat suddenly redoubled; and altogether, the proceedings took on the nightmare aspect of a surrealist film. Happily, two decades of domesticity had taught me how to cope with such family crises. Immuring myself in the powder room of the flying machine, I permitted myself just enough hysterics to calm and refresh me, painted my trachea with brandy, and reappeared a confident, well-organized personality. Within the six-hour flight to Bangkok, I managed, by a judicious mixture of sophistry and Hennessey, to convince my helpmate that life without flat silver was not insupportable, and recklessly vowing that if we ever struck another thrift shop I would replace her service ten times over, passed out cold.

Only a distaste for unnecessary sadism prevents me from recounting the ordeal in which, during the days that ensued, I found shelter in Bangkok for four bodies and twenty-one pieces of luggage. To anyone inclined to scoff at our plight, I can merely echo the trenchant words of the Beard of Avon, viz., that he jests at scars that never felt a wound. Because of the war in China and Siam's relative prosperity, the capital had been evolving since 1947 into a crossroads of commerce and was completely chock-a-block. Every available bed had been pre-empted by legation staffs and business panjandrums evacuated from Shanghai, fantastic premiums were being offered for the veriest lean-to, and the one vacancy in town, the snake pit at the Pasteur Institute untenanted after the death of their hamadryad, was too cramped for my quartet. Under the circumstances, the stash I finally ferreted out was a windfall. It was a modest, ramshackle pension in the Thung Mahamek district, operated by a Frenchwoman popularly credited with having been the plaything of Ivar Kreuger. Madame Sauvage may indeed have tiptoed through the Wamsutta with the Swedish match king, but I rather suspect she fostered the myth to give her premises glamour. A slightly overblown peony in a bush-jacket that unsuccessfully struggled to conceal her charms, she had the lazy, mascaraed come-hither of the whole generation of vamps typified by Valeska Suratt and Clara Kimball Young. Our fellow boarders were out of a later, post-Biograph epoch, but they were equally calculated to warm the cockles of Alfred Hitchcock's heart. To mention but four who came and went, there was an introspective French archaeologist who sold shoe-polish and vitamin capsules on the side; an ebullient Jugoslav acting as agent for a Swiss bicycle firm; a disputatious Dutch accountant with a roomful of bar-bells and punching-bags, and a woebegone Portuguese vice-consul who had fallen out of favor at Lisbon, and like a policeman banished to Staten Island, was pounding the diplomatic beat in Southeast Asia.

The first item on the agenda, naturally, was orienting the family to its new surroundings. This entailed a program of sightseeing, afternoon calls, and dinner parties I could have cheerfully dispensed with, but the fat was in the fire and I bared my throat to the knife with as much grace as I could muster. The kindest thing that can be said for the social life of the American colony in Bangkok is that nobody has ever died of ennui, though there were times when I felt like a very poor insurance risk. To be trapped helplessly at a dinner table between two Gorgon-faced matrons discussing revers and faggoting, while your collar wilts in the overpowering heat and mosquitoes batten on your legs, is a form of martyrdom that no early Christian father was ever called on to endure. Many of my compatriots, particularly the newer embassy crowd, were living on an extremely dickty scale; they had grandiose establishments, whole corps of servants, outriders and lackeys innumerable, and similar juicy perquisites, a circumstance which occasionally tempted them to behave like demigods and hand down magisterial judgments. Over the walnuts and wine, they were given to teetering on their heels and spouting pompous rubbish that made the toes curl with embarrassment. Most of it was a warmed-over hash of what they had read in *Time* or *Reader's Digest,* salted with the Princetonian self-esteem that flourishes in the foreign service. 1 decided I had met my Waterloo the night a twenty-two-year-old graduate of the Pentagon

Front elevation, Bangkok.

raised his glass and proposed a toast to the greatest American since Lincoln, Henry Luce. From then on, I dined in Chinese cook-shops, snatching a bowl of bean sprouts or a filet of squid on the wing. The food was far less plushy, but the dialogue was also considerably less fraught with heartburn.

Generally speaking, Bangkok was pretty much as I remembered it from two years before, a pleasant hodge-podge of metropolis and village, interlarded with temples, waterways swarming with sampans, and an agreeable polyglot population. Nevertheless, a pronounced change had taken place in the interval; the shaky dictatorship of Pibul Songgram, tightening its grip after two unsuccessful coups d'état, and the Nationalist collapse in the South China provinces, had produced a bumper harvest of tensions and anxieties in everyday life. Road-blocks, civilian search, and military surveillance of automobiles were now accepted as normal, and it was more and more apparent that behind its bucolic façade, Siam was fast flowering into a fairly nasty little police state. I am not altogether certain when the first faint canker of disillusion began gnawing at me, but I awoke one morning some weeks after our arrival with a small Rhode Island millstone, approximately twelve feet across, resting squarely on my chest. The air inside the mosquito netting was as heavy as flannel and through the room swirled the pervasive stench of canal mud which is one of the minor blessings of Bangkok. To my surprise, the queen bee was propped upright in bed, immersed in a travel folder. The instant she felt my gaze, she attempted to bury the leaflet under her pillow, but not before I saw that it dealt with the French Riviera.

"So that's what's been going on behind my back," I breathed. "Where'd you get that?"

"Out of your top bureau drawer, where you hid it under those pornographic postcards," she returned. "Listen, I'm sick of this cat-and-mouse game. Why don't we both come clean?"

"You—you mean you're tired of Bangkok?" I asked evasively.

"Of course not, silly boy," she said, disentangling a lizard from her hair and tossing it into the commode. "I think it's the prettiest place I've ever seen—next to Woodlawn Cemetery, that is. I love the long, steamy afternoons of lounging in this teakwood stall with the sweat cascading down my frame, the voluptuous nights of swapping cake recipes with army wives and fly-specked gallantries with their husbands, the whole vibrant pattern of colonial suburbia. It's like life in an antiquated fireless cooker."

"The kids are happy here, though," I said feebly. "I mean, they haven't tried to drown themselves or anything, have they?"

"They're too bushed," she said. "They're so done up with the heat they've stopped kicking each other, and Snookums, that's a bad sign."

"You know, dear," I observed, clearing my throat tentatively, "I didn't want to upset you heretofore, but I've been over to the Hindu soothsayers in Suriwong Road, and—well, I'm afraid they gave me some pretty momentous news."

"You're going to take a long trip," she hazarded, with

137

that peculiar feminine clairvoyance science is at such a
loss to explain. "Did they say anything about a tall,
dark-tempered brunette and two children?"

"Why, no," I confessed. "Of course, I only got the
two-bit horoscope."

"Next time buy the economy family size," she recommended, "or better still, give me the quarter. I can read
you like a book." Significantly enough, from the moment
the cat was out of the bag and the yoke of self-imposed
exile lifted from our necks, our spirits rocketed. Bangkok, once we had ruthlessly exorcised the obligation to
linger in it, immediately became picturesque again; the
quaint, teeming thoroughfares had never seemed so
romantic, and our friends, enraptured by the knowledge
that we were only a temporary nuisance, smothered us
with conviviality. Infused with fresh vitality, we dedicated ourselves to oiling the machinery of departure.
My share of the labor was soon accomplished; I escorted
my letter of credit to the air booking office, paced the
anteroom feverishly while it was given a spinal and de-
livered of four inky tickets to Istanbul, Rome, and Nice,
and left it in a local pawnshop for fresh plasma to ease
the postoperative shock. The mem and children, mean-
while, systematically winnowed every novelty shop and
curio bazaar in the five-mile length of the New Road,
disinterring undreamt-of treasures—cravats woven of
snakeskin, model junks that glowed in the dark, porcelain umbrella jars, and a collection of walking sticks,
parasols, and riding crops that would make our attic the
peer of any in Pennsylvania. Preparations were going

forward apace and our acquisitions overflowed two hangars at the airport when a chance remark of Madame Sauvage over the dinner table wrought new complications.

"Why don't you take back a pet for the little ones?" she suggested. "A Korat cat or a gibbon to remind them of the exciting days they passed in Thailand."

"His check stubs'll do that," commented my wife affectionately. "With nowhere as many fleas."

"What you need is a mynah bird," broke in Mr. Krosig, the Balkan roomer. "It never stays still from morning to night. All the time chattering and whistling and imitating the various sounds."

"Ah, the old crab would shut it off the way he does my radio," grumbled my son. The old crab gave him a look that singed three buttons off his jumper and switched the conversation to the large number of boys annually eaten by werewolves. Mr. Krosig, who had been in Transylvania and had some pertinent data on the subject, took it up avidly, and I thought I had effectively disposed of the matter until my daughter commenced needling me. She would forgo her allowance for the next eight years if I only bought a mynah; she would go to second-rate boarding schools, bleach her own hair, live on scraps, weave her own clothing. Ultimately, badgered into submission, I capitulated. A circuit of the bird market revealed plenty of mynahs, but none sufficiently glossy and articulate. At last, outside a Chinese firecracker store, we discovered a specimen endowed with purple plumage, a primrose-yellow comb,

Outside a Chinese firecracker store, we discovered
a specimen endowed with purple plumage.

a spirited eye, and a reasonably fluent vocabulary of Siamese invective. The asking price of fifty ticals, approximately two and a half dollars, was pure formality; before the dicker was sealed, I had been conned into buying five bags of Roman candles and pinwheels, a mandarin coat, and two tins of preserved lychee nuts. Whatever Tong Cha's shortcomings as a room-mate—he rose with the sun and exercised his repertory until the last eardrum cried uncle—, he was a match-less antidote for tedium poisoning. I spent the two days prior to our take-off gyrating about Bangkok for health certificates to transport him to Europe, sub-ordinated comfort and sanity to outfitting him with a proper cage, securing a special bird's-size ticket and visas, and assembling his food, a balanced regimen of rice, chili peppers, bananas, and hard-boiled eggs. He demonstrated his worth beyond cavil, however, and in a fashion that left no doubt about his intelligence. When the Siamese exit customs closed in and started to bur-row through our effects in the usual search for cocaine and Annamite girls, he sprayed them with a shower of Sanskrit cuss-words that reduced them to jelly. He never told me what he said, but if I could learn the English equivalent, my name would rank with that of Rabelais.

Inside the dimly lit cabin of the Constellation dron-ing toward Calcutta, I lay wrapped in a blissful, air-conditioned Nirvana, somnolently intent on one of the truly enduring contributions to Western technology, the smoothly undulating haunches of the hostess as she moved up the aisle administering to the needy. Perhaps, I thought drowsily, I had been the victim of a major error the past five months; perhaps the air-foam seat I sat in, the aromatic coffee I sipped, and that brave vibration each way free, as Herrick had so succinctly put it, were worth all the tea in China. Was I an epicene old goat that I should be content to nibble among the ivory, apes, and peacocks of a moribund continent, or, after all, a mettlesome middle-aged goat whose hoofs Nature had designed to twinkle from as yet unexplored crags? I thought of asking my wife, sleeping peacefully beside me, but I could pretty well envision her answer. Let the morrow bring what it would, I decided, as our motorized kite slid across the Bay of Bengal and I cuddled closer to the Sandman. Buddha might get me in the last great round-up, but for the moment, Baby was still on the range.

9

Pickle-Puss in Seven-League Boots

CHAKRI LAL, THIRD assistant passenger agent of the Calcutta branch of Indian Airways, sleepily dismounted from the bone-shaker on which he had pedaled to the airport, snapped shut its bicycle lock, and languidly scratching his fundament to awaken the circulatory system, ambled into the waiting room. His habitual morning melancholy, aggravated by a collision with a chicken en route to the field, had put him in a funereal humor; in the untimely death of the fowl, which had cost him two rupees and a savage dressing-

143

down from a constable, he saw the portent of a disastrous day, brimful of nagging superiors, passenger complaints, and petty exasperations. The premonition increased when he caught sight of the four Europeans dozing amid their luggage in the transient section. They were evidently members of the same tribal unit, for they lay cradled higgledy-piggledy against each other, breathing stertorously through their open mouths, and their disheveled hand-me-downs bore a uniform dingy patina of travel. Rumanian gypsies, probably some itinerant party of horse-thieves and coppersmiths, decided Chakri Lal, after a cursory glance at the mother of the family, a swarthy but personable matron bedecked with rings. Then his eye jumped to the unmistakable T-shirts of the children, the mosaic of portable typewriter, short-wave radio, and Far Eastern loot which he knew to be the hallmark of the Yankee nomad. The agent groaned. In another few minutes, they would begin stirring about and clamoring for all manner of things unprocurable—sowbelly and grits, ice-cream sundaes, aureomycin. As he glumly appraised their suitcases, wondering in his fatalistic way how many he would be accused of pilfering before they emplaned, he noticed at their feet a curious object, some two feet square and swathed in black cloth. Approaching it stealthily, he raised a corner of the curtain and peeped underneath. Immediately the air was rent with a fearful piercing screech, and Chakri Lal, his nose neatly dimpled by the beak of a mynah bird (*Gracula javanensis*), catapulted backward into the lap of the narrator.

He raised a corner of the curtain
and peeped underneath.

To be struck in the pit of the stomach by a flying Hindu is, on the whole, a form of reveille inferior to the peal of distant chimes or the caresses of a Circassian odalisque. Coming on top of four hours' slumber in a room so stifling that beads of mercury stood out on the thermometer, it might well have proved fatal. Notwithstanding, I did not permit my spleen to get the better of me (mainly because Chakri Lal had splintered it with his impact), and brushing him good-humoredly to the floor, I proceeded to organize my dependents into some semblance of chaos. Circumstances had conspired to aid me. The day before, the airline ferrying us to Istanbul had been enjoined by the authorities from operating over India. This meant that we would have to cross the peninsula in a model plane powered by rubber bands to Karachi, where we might resume the trip aboard a Constellation. Words—at least antiseptic ones —cannot convey what a pyramid of questionnaires, certificates, vouchers, receipts, affidavits, and credentials the switch entailed, what niggling scrutiny of passports, haggling over surcharges, and Talmudic boggling over minutiae like the mynah's precise weight. Throughout these formalities, the youngsters thought it best to unpack all the seashells they had collected in the Moluccas and display them to bystanders, while the bird, egged on by a crowd of excited porters, manfully strove to dash out his brains against the bars of his cage. It was a scene as full of color and movement as Rosa Bonheur's *Horse Fair*, and as I drank in its myriad shifting details, I longed to get it down on canvas, roll it into a tube, and touch a match to it.

The hop to New Delhi, in a superannuated Viking transport jammed with Parsee merchants, was dire enough to justify our forebodings, though nobody could have predicted two minor bits of fantasy that embellished it. The first was a flight breakfast to end flight breakfasts, consisting of great greasy pastry-shells the size of Patrick Henry's tricorne filled with cold vegetable curry, cookies stamped out of an elderly Kashmir sweater and frosted with its buttons, mildewed cashew nuts, and barley-sugar candies washed down with warm lemon soda. The other was a technical gimmick entirely new to me, and, I suspect, unique in commercial aviation. Attached to the usual indicator that flashes "No Smoking" and "Fasten Seat Belts" was a special panel which suddenly rapped out the provocative bulletin, "Toilet Engaged." Whether this stop-press extra was designed to curb excessive traffic in the aisles, or merely to signify that someone had retired for a fast drag of hashish, the steward refused to divulge. He did intimate in demotic Hindustani, however, that his silence had been purchased by a little group of unscrupulous men in whose interest it was to keep such information from the public. I knew better than to press the matter, for too many Nosey Parkers given to asking embarrassing questions had already been found floating in the Brahmaputra, and it needed no great imagination to discern behind a trembling pawn the familiar lineaments of Professor Moriarty and Colonel Sebastian Moran.

Our fatuous supposition that we would continue to

A special panel suddenly rapped out the bulletin, "Toilet Engaged."

Karachi on the same plane was, of course, deflated at Delhi; we were bundled into the customs area, again put through the whole *Walpurgisnacht* of inspection and weighing, and transferred to an ancient Dakota whose floor was slippery with betel juice. The rest of the day was epochal, a mixture of the monotonous and the gruesome. The aircraft bucked consumptively across the limitless eroded wastes of Pakistan, now dropping in abrupt cataclysmic descents, now belted skyward by air currents from the baking gorges below. The faces of the passengers, present company included, grew greener by the hour; in the seat behind us, a heavily veiled Moslem woman, traveling in purdah, besought Allah in unceasing strangled sobs to deliver her from misery. Even Tong Cha, stowed in his cage at the rear of the compartment, had fallen mute and, in the classic pose associated with Madame Récamier, lay staring dully at an overturned water-cooler. Jodhpur, the only break in the flight, was a furnace. We reeled through the 114-degree heat to a darkened resthouse and sat befuddled at tables that burned the fingers, unable to grasp how the human mechanism can function in such surroundings. Yet it does, and gaudily; the last thing one sees as the city recedes under the fuselage is the tremendous air-conditioned palace of the Maharajah which was fifteen years in building—a monument of misdirected energy, admittedly, but a still greater tribute to the stamina of his subjects.

The next twenty-four hours were as insubstantial and elusive of description as one of Little Nemo's Welsh rabbit dreams. Out of it I retain little but the memory of bone-breaking fatigue, unshaven border officials pawing impatiently through passports, and a few scattered images: a labyrinthine hotel at Karachi where the roar of airplane motors made sleep a travesty, the interminable stony expanse of Iraq and the equally stony visages of its police at Basra, a tiny lunchroom at Damascus of surpassing filth and turbulence whose tea and biscuits comprised the only nourishment we were served between the Persian Gulf and Istanbul. It was somewhat ironic that for all the breezy literature the airline persistently sprinkled on the customer, extolling its service in the frolicsome language copywriters dote on, nobody should have bothered to provide a cup of bouillon or a potato chip to allay his hunger. The children became so ravenous at length that I was reduced to steeping in hot water an inspirational leaflet of the company describing its superb flight meals. It made a weak saccharine infusion which temporarily appeased their pangs, but if I ever wing through the Middle East under the same auspices, I shall take care to arm myself with a haggis, a bag of pemmican, or a couple of bloaters.

Istanbul, as far as I know, has never inflamed the songsmiths of Tin-Pan Alley; the Swanee holds a preferred position in their hearts to the Bosporus, and offhand I cannot recall any tearful supplications in their ballads to carry them back to dear old Byzantium. Nevertheless, there are few cities more soothing to the eye of the spent traveler who has just issued from the cauldron of India. It was a cool spring afternoon as we jolted through the outskirts in an ancient airport bus; sheep grazed among the ruined fortifications in the rolling hills, and on the whitewashed latticework of small outdoor cafés, magnificent purple wisteria was just coming into bloom. The crowds surging along the main thoroughfare displayed a vitality and purposefulness we had not encountered since San Francisco. They boiled by the hundreds on the sidewalks outside the cinemas, gorged themselves on flamboyant mocha and pistachio tarts in the ice-cream parlors, milled around barrows laden with sesame seed, halvah, and nougat. The blood magically began flowing in our veins again. Released from months of tropical inertia, I gave my heirs a resounding box on the ear to apprise them that I was doing business at the old stand and that I was prepared to deal summarily with any juvenile infractions, actual or fancied. My wife, who had occasioned us considerable anxiety for several days by neglecting to berate me, likewise emerged from her coma. Exercising an unrivaled talent for hyperbole, she denounced my irresponsibility in bringing two hapless infants into a strange city in the dead of night without a hotel reservation.

"I know this place," she whimpered. "It's full of Macedonian morphine peddlers and raddled soubrettes stealing submarine plans from Orson Welles; I saw it all in *A Coffin for Dimitrios*. You wait, this Don Quixote won't be happy till he's got us sleeping in a repossessed mosque." Her misgivings, it goes without saying, were totally unfounded. After only three hours of entreaty and bribery, punctuated by the mynah's deafening cries, we bivouacked in a crumbling old flytrap reminiscent of a Forty-seventh Street theatrical hotel, rich with red plush and dusty palms. The lobby made up in atmosphere whatever comfort the rooms lacked; there was always a quorum of furtive-eyed raisin merchants from Smyrna whispering hypothetical deals or buxom ladies of the town, redolent of attar of roses, rolling their liquid eyes in invitation. Everyone was immoderately cordial and ready to help—too much so, in fact, for I twice surprised my son in badinage with the Turkish lassies, twirling his adolescent mustaches like a heavy dragoon. If I had not sent him packing and myself taken the coryphees into the bar to lecture them severely on their shamelessness, his gallantries might have had a disastrous outcome.

Once we had complied with the tedious etiquette of shuffling around the Suleyman and Blue Mosques in carpet slippers and left enough baksheesh in Santa Sophia to gild the transept, sightseeing became noisome and we wandered wherever fancy dictated. There is probably no place in the world more ideally suited to the purpose than the Grand Bazaar, the great underground warren in which the Emperor Constantine is reputed to have stabled his forty thousand chargers. The detritus of every civilization since the tenth century clogs its miles of stalls; you can buy Saracen armor, early Victor talking-machines with brass horns, jeweled Russian ikons, Boer War puttees, onyx boxes, primitive Negro statuary, electric vibrators, worthless oil stock, *ceintures de chastité,* and furniture, rugs, lamps, tapestries, paintings, and porcelains that would make the loose-wristed sodality of Third Avenue perish with desire. For those seeking interior decoration in a stricter sense, there were culinary treasures at the restaurant named Pandelis near by: the delicate pasties known as *borek,* the various savory shish kebabs impaled on spears, and that stellar dessert, *ecmed kadayif,* a sonnet of ambrosial shortbread surmounted by clotted cream. Our single dip into Istanbul's night life was nowhere as rewarding. Hip by thigh with eighty other gulls, we sat in a fetid, smoky boîte recommended as the ultimate in sophisticated entertainment. The star turn was a chemically blond French chanteuse, all verve and impassioned gestures, in whose songs the words *chagrin, désir,* and *crépuscule* recurred with dingdong regularity. It is my contention that if these three terms were stricken from the French language, the effect would be as tonic as the fall of the Bastille. The whole genus of visceral contralto would be driven back to the kitchen to make soup, which is its true talent, and its victims freed to play klabiatsch or to listen to Abe Burrows, the only cultivated pastimes left to twentieth-century man.

Though no city as multifaceted as Istanbul can yield much but fragmentary impressions in the space of a week, the portion we saw was altogether beguiling. Reviewing it aboard the Panair Do Brasil plane bearing us onward to Rome, each of us cherished his own pleasurable recollection. My son dwelt wistfully on the oxidized silver Arabian dueling pistols in the Grand Bazaar and the similarly oxidized maidens in the hotel lobby; my daughter yearned for the multitude of majestic Angora cats we had cruelly denied her; my wife grew lyrical over an emerald necklace which some plausible Greek swore he had glommed from the Grand Duchess Olga's throat with his own hands. I myself recalled an idyllic cruise to Prinkipo in the Sea of Marmora, the white gingerbread villas overlooking its secluded coves, the fragrant pine-shaded roads we had traversed in a creaking old surrey, the Crimean War barracks and the minarets across the sparkling bay, the compulsion to hide away in this corner so immeasurably remote from the singing commercial and the Gallup poll. The difficulty was that unlike Trotsky, its most distinguished exile, I was no political refugee or polemicist, and short of drinking myself to death, I couldn't possibly imagine how to while away the days there—outside Burrows and klabiatsch, of course, which might conceivably pall.

Only some scientific wizard like Alessandro Volta, equipped with sensitive instruments and a knowledge of the explosive Italian temperament, could have calculated the electric effect of our arrival upon the Roman customs control. Confronted with sixty-seven cartons of American cigarettes, an Indo-Chinese passerine bird, five Buddha heads, and a score of other outlandish novelties, their hysteria attained a truly operatic pitch. Within five minutes, everything we owned, down to my daughter's dental braces, was confiscated, frisked, returned, and confiscated again. I was finally offered the choice of paying $325 or having the cigarettes im-

Ordeal by hysteria: the Roman customs control.

pounded until our departure. I agreed to the latter on condition that they impound the mynah as well, but after examining him minutely, they decided he would not be as edible as the larks and linnets they were accustomed to and refused. It was a shrewd maneuver on my part, since if I had tried to hustle him through as a lawful member of my entourage, he most certainly would have wound up that evening *cacciatora* style, in a bed of pimentos.

In three years of vagabondage, I have rarely met with fawning and groveling to surpass our reception at the Palazzo Diplomatico, the grandiose pile on the Via Veneto that gave us shelter. That we had fallen among brigands of the deepest dye was manifest at once; every matchbook, toothpick, and sliver of toast borne to us on silver salvers was entered four times in the bill and as copiously peppered with surtaxes as a broadtail coat. Inasmuch as the spring tourist rush had forced us into a de luxe hotel, we were resigned to being robbed blind, but the wolfishness, the orgiastic delirium with which we were taken to the cleaners, gave piracy a new dimension. Beneath his braided exterior, reminiscent of Emil Jannings in *The Last Laugh*, the head porter of the Diplomatico concealed an effrontery greater than Texas Guinan's; when I branded sixty-seven dollars an exorbitant fee for a five-word cable to the States, he loftily explained that it had been routed by way of Baffin's Bay and that only a piker or a Communist would cavil at the cost of a team of huskies. As I backed away stammering apologies, he swept open his ledger and clipped me twelve hundred lire for geographic information and zoology charges.

While Rome's chief concern was still religious pilgrims and trippers, and the same old hurly-burly of college boys, spinsters, and monks packed the Piazza Espagna trading their dollars to black marketeers, a new voice was loud in the land, that of the movie entrepreneur. The nascent picture industry had drawn to the Eternal City a stampede of Hollywood agents, talent scouts, gossip columnists, and related succubi; in the fashionable bars below the Borghese Gardens, pudgy men in hand-painted ties and suède oomphies overwhelmed each other with superlatives, and the idler who paused to lace his shoe was likely to find himself immortalized in the next documentary film. The fever had also gripped the citizenry, thousands of whom had been promised jobs in an impending five-million-dollar production of *Quo Vadis* and thereupon had quit work to loaf about learnedly discussing the love life of Anna Magnani. Sadly enough, the project blew up because of an unforeseen felon on Gregory Peck's thumb, plunging the populace into gloom worse than that following the news of the retreat from Caporetto. So many I.O.U.'s were destroyed that in the resultant snowstorm, rubberneck parties had to be conveyed to St. Peter's and the Roman Forum in pungs.

On an intensive diet of various lethal pastas like fettucini, ravioli, spaghetti, and green noodles, it was not very long before the poundage the family had shed in the Orient returned with interest. Sporting the stylish pneumatic tire of fat around our middles known as the canelloni roll, we flexed our stringy muscles and bravely faced up to the task of cleansing our satchels of the old shinplasters which clogged them. It was a Herculean undertaking, but the Roman shopkeepers worked like navvies to assist us, asking no reward for themselves but a paltry six hundred per cent. With their sympathetic guidance, we collected the wagonloads of Florentine leather book-ends and polychrome candlesticks, the wrought-iron sconces and pious bric-a-brac, that are indispensable adjuncts to gracious living. On the final afternoon of our five-day stopover, it looked for a tense moment as though we might still be solvent when we left; but I resourcefully met the challenge by acquiring an entire set of matched rawhide luggage I had no earthly use for and then flung our remaining currency from the roof of the Barberini palace—a gesture which did much to ratify the Italian conviction that the American tourist was no Scrooge but a liberal, open-handed fellow and paved the way toward genuine understanding between the two nations.

In the rows of chairs lining the Boulevard des Anglais at Nice, the respectable widowed ladies in maline hats and the aging British remittance men who exist nowhere else sunned themselves in their immemorial fashion exactly where I had left them a couple of years before. I craned my neck out the taxi window and ticked off the buildings as they flashed by: the Negresco, its candy-box facade glistening under fresh white paint, the

West-End, the Casino spruced up for the summer visitors, the Ruhl as forbidding as a fortress. I was about to dash away a tear at the memories they aroused when I abruptly realized they held none; they were just a lot of noisy real estate in which I had been effectively skinned in the past. How much more satisfactory to be bound for a tranquil hamlet like Beaulieu-sur-Mer, amid whose peaceful, flowering byways we could be quietly mulcted by experts. Gears grinding, the taxi began the slow, toilsome ascent of the hill toward Villefranche; I looked back at the rest of my family, unable to ride with me because of our massive baggage, gamely trotting in my wake with their tongues lolling out.

"Suck in your paunches there!" I called encouragingly. "Only a few miles more!" They nodded dumbly and quickened their pace. I lay back, lit a cigarette, and with the cool wind of the Mediterranean stirring my hair, surrendered myself to dreams.

10

How Much Lotus Can You Eat?

T HE CHURCH BELLS of Beaulieu-sur-Mer at the foot of the French Maritime Alps had just finished striking noon as Solange, the manicurist of the town's principal barbershop, yawned and tossed aside the issue of *Cinémonde* in which she had been reading Jean Gabin's adjuration to his fans to keep their glands youthful. She snorted contemptuously. A pretty state of affairs when any Frenchman needed such prompting, she thought, stripping her smock from a figure that had made Beaulieu, from a glandular standpoint, one of the more stimulating spots along the Mediterranean. She gave her brassy metallic marcel a reassuring pat, twisted a stocking seam slightly so that she could readjust it in front of the meat market and give the butcher a thrill, and pushed through the bead curtain enclosing her cubicle. The last of the morning's clients, a prognathous foreigner with a tonsure resembling a Franciscan friar's, was hunched down in a chair having his neck shaved by Michel, the hairdresser who handled patrons from the local hotels.

"*Tiens,* are you still grooming that camel?" she snorted. "Listen, nobody can make a silk *porte-monnaie* out of a sow's *oreille.*"

"Well, he looks better than he did," said Michel, scraping away at the customer as though he were holy-stoning a deck. "You should have seen him when

"Tiens, *are you grooming that camel?*" she sno

his wife and children brought him in here. I thought
he was an anchorite or fakir until I hacked through the
foliage."

"What is he, an Irish?" asked Solange. Her eyes lit up
hopefully. "Regard well, he has a Celtic appearance like
that embezzler the gendarmes are offering a reward
for."

"No, worse luck," said Michel. "Just an American
spendthrift who's been kicking around Africa with his
family."

"Not Africa—the extreme Orient," I corrected over
my shoulder, "and since you've gone ahead and cropped
my right eyebrow, please delete the other one to corre-
spond."

"*Mot de Cambronne,*" stammered Michel, reddening
to his widow's peak. "Am I to understand that Monsieur
comprehends French?"

"Enough to field those Texas leaguers you've been
blooping at me," I grunted. "All right, make with the
talc already and slip off my gyves."

"Graciously, my general," he breathed, all sugary
smiles. "You have but to command." Sprinkling a handful of hair down my back to cool the spine, he enveloped
me in a mist of brilliantine and rice powder and whisked
off the apron. The apparition that greeted me from the
mirror on donning my prisms was unnerving. I beheld
a shifty-eyed Apache with pointed sideburns and a tight
spit-curl roached down over his villainous forehead, the
sort of furtive gunsel named René-the-Hypo whom the
authorities believe was seen lurking around the villa

prior to the jewel theft. The effect was so crippling to the ego that I inadvertently shelled out five francs less than my usual tip, or a total of seven cents, and mantling my head in a Napoleonic dicer improvised from a copy of *Le Figaro,* slunk back to the hotel.

It was almost four weeks since I had steered my troupe, hollow-eyed, pinch-nostriled, and dog-tired, into the Hôtel Cafard on the coast facing the promontory of Cap Ferrat, and our corporate metabolism was only now beginning to recover the buckram it had lost east of Suez. With a voracity that left the waiters aghast and reduced the manager to speechless rage, we kept tamping down the bountiful table d'hôte and clamoring for more; between meals, the children ran from the *épicerie* to the English tearoom, stuffing themselves with croissants, bath buns, and lethal raspberry ices. The memsahib and I, publicly scorning their grossness, were craftier. We hid bags of croissants, pâté de foie gras, sardines, anchovies, and cognate delicatessen under a loose floor board, and crammed our bellies in midnight beanos that would have shamed the Tennessee Shad and Doc MacNooder. Twice we were nearly betrayed by Tong Cha, our mynah bird, who, scenting the goodies, screeched and brought the bairns running in to confront us with our mouths full. After I spiked his rice with a quarter grain of nembutal, however, and slipped them the same for good measure, the meddling ceased and our gluttony was truly unbridled.

Life at the Cafard was by and large uneventful; the seasonal tourist avalanche had not yet hit the Riviera,

The irreducible minimum known as the rasurel.

and outside a biweekly busload of Danish giantesses who smoked cheroots and ducked each other boisterously in the Mediterranean, the guests were mainly clandestine weekend couples and spidery young British actors in gay neckcloths. Everyone spent his waking hours on the strip of beach before the hotel, mangling his feet on the shifting pebbles or doggedly frying his midriff an angry scarlet in a vain effort to appear eupeptic. The French bathing suit, it was instructive to note, had been sheared down from my last memory of it to the irreducible minimum known as the Rasurel, a microscopic triangle laced across the hips and supplemented in the womenfolk by an extremely sketchy bandeau. While undeniably hygienic, it was a costume demanding the flawless proportions of a Nita Naldi or Earle Liederman, and it was utterly merciless on anybody cursed with sheepshanks or a prolapsed stomach, as were most of those who affected it. But excessive self-consciousness has never been a Latin frailty, and what might have aroused stupefaction elsewhere was here considered merely *sportif*. This was especially the case with a young blood who appeared dramatically one day for an afternoon's spear-fishing, escorted by a sizable retinue of attendants, masseurs, relatives, and well-wishers. He wore demi-Bikini shorts, rubber flippers on his hands and feet, a Cyclops underwater goggle with periscope attachment, and a wire like a zoot chain for receiving his catch. Brandishing the tubeful of poisoned arrows with which he manifestly planned to strike down his prey, he made a lengthy, declamatory speech of fare-

167

well, drank two Cinzanos, and having shaken hands all around, sallied gingerly into the water. The crowd watched tensely, shouting warnings and encouragement to the intrepid one as he plunged deeper. At about waist height, he turned, waved a final goodbye, and submerged. In all he remained below about four minutes, with three reappearances to draw breath. Then, puffing like a grampus (a grampus was puffing near by, so that I had some basis for comparison), he staggered back to shore amid wild acclaim for his escape from a watery grave, announced that there were no fish to be had, embraced each member of the gallery in turn, drank another apéritif, and was triumphantly borne off to the café to relate his adventures, which, it was plain, bade fair to eclipse anything in Jules Verne.

Take one Nirvana with another, our choice of Beaulieu as a haven to career in and chip the barnacles from our keels was fairly lucky. It was quiet, tidy, and, above all, devoid of the Asbury Park *Schweinerei*, the concentration of beachwear shops, pseudo-nautical bars, and frenetic casinos that had mushroomed at places like Saint Tropez, La Condamine, and Bandol. On our few forays into the latter, they all turned out to be full of intense young men in blue rope espadrilles and surrealist chin-whiskers squabbling about Jean-Paul Sartre; where once the fishermen had spread their seines were now boogie-woogie and fried clams. Emotional Francophiles love to contend that it was American influence that cheapened the Riviera; to my way of thinking, the fault lay with the French vacationists themselves, who no longer seemed capable of sipping a vermouth without a radio blasting a light cavalry overture in the background and whose sartorial lunacies surpassed anything at Palm Springs. Beaulieu, as a matter of fact, was an ideal grandstand seat to observe them at their most unhinged. From the sidewalk of the Bristol bar any evening, you could watch them roar along the Lower Corniche in explosive hot-rods piled with household effects, crash helmets askew on their heads and lips skinned back with the diabolic application of such boyhood heroes as Ralph di Palma or Teddy Tetzlaff. They were on their way to Monaco to eat custard apples on a stick and dance *le jitterbug,* and God help anyone who gainsaid them.

Normally, it would have taken a tidal wave to wrench us out of so sybaritic an existence and force our feet to the road again, but a seed I had rashly planted in Siam two months earlier now bore fruit and we had to depart to England to harvest it. In a moment of paranoia, I had gone off the deep end and acquired a small British sports car for delivery in London about midsummer, the design being to round off our global jaunt with a leisurely circuit of Great Britain and the Continent. The expense would be piffling, I assured myself; indeed, the whole operation was a tremendous economy, as we would save rail fares, sleep in quaint old inns, dine al fresco off a bit of bread and cheese, etc., etc. How I ever arrived at this specious reasoning is rather unclear, but it was unquestionably a combination of sunstroke and the state classified by psychologists as *folie de grandeur.*

At any rate, the day after word arrived that our little Moon-Glow was weaned and awaited adoption, we entrained for Marseilles. My purpose in going there was dual: to test at first hand its world-famous bouillabaisse and its equally renowned ptomaine, and to show the youngsters the Château d'If as an example of what befell people who were lippy to their fathers. The moral lesson unfortunately went sour when the guide of the prison accidentally blabbed to the children that Edmond Dantès had wound up with millions and a title. From that day forward, my life became a hell.

Our stay in Paris was little more than a glancing blow, owing to the record-breaking tourist influx and the resultant scarcity of accommodations; the American Express boiled like the floor of the Chicago wheat pit with crew haircuts and seersucker, and the only French audible at the Deux Magots and the Café Flore was out of the mouths of babes from Bennington and sucklings from Swarthmore. The two rooms I had chiseled by bribery and tears from a decrepit hotel in the Carrefour du Bac were so exquisitely dingy that they might have served as a stage set. The massive dusty draperies, the bilious wallpaper, the armoires of fake pearwood veneer, and the ghostly smell of hair-oil and generations of traveling salesmen from Lyon would have made a perfect locale for one of those Grand Guignol romps in which the characters skewer each other with hatpins. The sole advantage of the quarters was an ample bay window where the mynah took his daily sun-bath. The building opposite housed some French ministry or other swarming with female clerks, and every time Tong Cha emitted his favorite ear-splitting wolf whistle, the ladies infallibly powdered their bugles and hung out over the sills, patently under the impression that the G.I.'s had reconquered the city.

The problem of keeping small fry amused in these unprepossessing surroundings was far from simple. For the first couple of days, they busied themselves adequately running the *ascenseur* and stalling it between floors, dropping bags of water on the passers-by, and stealing the manager's wig. Then the grim specter of ennui which stalks every child made its appearance and they started to pluck fretfully at our apron strings, chanting that ominous, disheartening refrain, "What'll we do na-a-ow?" A chance encounter resolved the dilemma; I ran across a minor police spy and cutthroat under whom I had studied blackmailing in 1927 and assigned him to conduct the kids on a tour of several suitable landmarks like the sewers of Paris, the Morgue, and the less fragrant stews of the rue Lépic. No dry-as-dust textbook could have prepared them so ably for the vicissitudes of later life. Under his direction, they learned the first principles of wielding a razor and the proper footwork of the *savate*, technical training that subsequently earned them an enviable ascendancy over their schoolmates. At the risk of sounding like the usual boastful parent, I know few adolescents today as adept at gouging out an opponent's eye at stick-ball or chewing off an ear in a scrimmage. What if they occasionally have to wear a muzzle or spend their holidays in the Tombs? At least they didn't turn into milksops.

171

The British customs being inflexibly opposed to the entry of tropical birds, we were compelled at this juncture to relinquish Tong Cha. I placed him with some misgivings in a *pension* for soft-billed orphans which I was positive would prove to be an avian version of Dotheboys Hall, but though he stood in peril of the birch and hazing, love had to give way to expediency. In the excitement of departure, I forgot to leave behind a can of worms, grubs, and flies we had laid in to vary his diet. Like the luckless Marches of Mr. Arlen's romance, we were never let off anything; at Hendon Airport outside London, the X-ray eye of His Majesty's inspector pounced on it among the welter of luggage and he demanded its nature.

"Why—uh—personal effects," I said hurriedly, seeking to dispense with a long complex explanation. "Titbits, you might say."

"What sort of titbits?" His face clearly registered suspicion that they were heroin crystals or uncut diamonds.

"Oh, just little—er—chewies," I squirmed. "The—the kiddies like to munch on them between meals."

"Let's have a dekko inside, shall we?" he proposed crisply. Twisting open the tin, he gaped into the interior and dropped it precipitately. As we filed into the airways bus, he stopped my daughter and handed her a half crown. "Here, spend that on fish and chips," he advised gruffly. "They're more liable to stick to the ribs."

Eleven days later, my wife stepped out of the front entrance of the Laburnum Court Hotel in Piccadilly and stood watching a scene that congealed her blood to ice. In the hot July sunshine, two harried bellboys and a foaming, overwrought creature she dimly recognized as her husband were struggling to lash a hillock of luggage to the rear of the Moon-Glow tourer at the curb. It was a handsome little vehicle, its red leather upholstery a rich contrast to the gleaming black body and smart canvas top, the high curving cowl flowing into the rakish cutaway doors, the dash sparkling with more mysterious gauges, meters, and indicators than a Wurlitzer organ. That it had cost her liege a small fortune and a week in the tortuous maze of British bureaucracy was relatively unimportant; what really concerned her was that it might also cost him an apoplectic seizure before the trip ever got started. In the end, my two assistant magicians and I somehow kicked, cuffed, and mashed the recalcitrant bags into submission, and the young, confined indoors with ear-stopples to cushion their sensibilities against Daddy's Elizabethan English, were stowed in the back seat. Followed by the speculative gaze of a number of morticians who had collected on the pavement, I slid under the right-hand drive, pulled on my gauntlets, and nosed into the tumultuous traffic of the West End.

Within the next twenty minutes, I learned under pressure the wisdom of two hoary adages, first, that you cannot teach an old dog raised on a Model T new tricks, and second, that a reflex in the hand is worth two in the clutch. The instant I found myself hemmed in by busses and lorries, wrestling a fantastic four-gear shift

*A scene that congealed
her blood to ice.*

I had never noticed before and driving the wrong way of the roadbed, I realized I had strayed too far from Walden Pond. As we careered crazily up Old Bond Street and through the Burlington Arcade (I seem to remember plowing from Fortnum & Mason's mackintosh section into the Reform Club, though there is no direct speedway linking the two), insurance rates rose to new highs in Hartford three thousand miles away. The other passengers, it need not be added, were at all times unstinting in their criticism and counsel; part of the way the machine steered itself while my palms were occupied in fanning life back into the children's breathless bodies. It must have been some uncanny animal intelligence built into the motor—the British are years ahead of us in matters mechanical—, that finally guided us out of the hubbub of Kensington into the Great West Road. Ninety miles ahead lay Bath, the spa Beau Nash and his fellow coxcombs had made illustrious and which, by tenanting for a night, we hoped to immortalize. In our haste, I stupidly neglected to burn the customary joss-sticks before undertaking the journey, an oversight that may have given offense to the ladies named Clotho, Lachesis, and Atropos who were weaving our destiny, because they almost put a crimp in it. A mile or so from our destination, nightfall and fatigue overtook me and I automatically swerved into the right-hand lane, square in the path of an onrushing express van. Again English technology rode to the rescue; so low-slung was the Moon-Glow that it passed smoothly under the housing of the truck without even grazing our top. All the same, it was a shattering experience, and none of us did more than pick at our fried plaice and gooseberry fool that evening.

At noon the next day, we were high in the lovely Wiltshire Downs, trying without success to carve our initials in the pillars of Stonehenge; it seems incredible that at this most historic of monuments, annually visited by thousands, neither crayons nor jackknife should be available for defacing the altar. The children, nevertheless, managed to scrawl a passable mustache on the Druid handling the ice-cream concession, and littering the grounds with popcorn and banana peels, we raced with renewed zest toward the southwest coast of Devon. It was drawing close to dusk when, grimy with dust and oil, we rolled up the graveled driveway of the Royal Weevil Hotel in Sidmouth, one of the lesser seaside resorts fringing the Channel. Our London friends had agreed that for a quiet fortnight in a genteel milieu, the Weevil was beyond cavil our cup of tea. The full ambiguity of the advice dawned on me as I surveyed the establishment; the rambling, gloomy building on the terraced lawn dotted with yews had the well-ordered look of an expensive sanitarium and the guests on the veranda were pointedly addressing themselves rather than their neighbors. Tiptoeing to the picture window in the ivy-covered gable, my wife and I stared in at a lounge where a handful of nonagenarians in steamer rugs were dipping Holland rusk into their cocoa with great deliberation.

"Is it all right?" she asked apprehensively. "Do you

The Moon-Glow passed smoothly under the housing of the truck.

think we can get breakfast in bed without hydrother-
apy?"

"Search me," I said. "It's sinister, but it's the only roof
this side of London." I looked around for my son.
"Where's Adam?"

"He's talking to some boys on the stoop," reported
his sister. "Here they come now." Arm in arm with two
fair-haired and altogether *soigné* lads of his own age
clad in blazers, my heir sauntered into view around the
corner.

"I say," remarked one of the newcomers, as his eyes
fell on the Moon-Glow. "What a simply wizard car."

"Oh, it serves for carrying out the ashes," agreed my
son nonchalantly.

"But who *are* those curious beggars around it?"

"Villagers, I daresay," said Adam, gazing right
through us. "Never saw the bleeders before in my life.
Well, come along, chaps, if we're to have a go at those
archery butts." The trio moved off down the greensward
out of sight. I took a step after them, opened my mouth
to speak, and closed it again. My wife laid a consoling
hand on my arm.

"It's just what you've always said, dear," she observed.
"There's nothing as broadening as travel."

11

Decorum, with Bread Sauce

WITH THE STUDIED CARE he always lavished on his postluncheon ritual, the maître d'hôtel of the Royal Weevil Hotel at Sidmouth, Devonshire, placed an infinitesimal speck of ash on the lapel of his cutaway, flicked an infinitesimal speck of ash from his lapel, shot his cuffs, checked his watch, and made a quick survey of the dining room. Only three tables were still occupied. A pair of crusty Anglo-Indians in mustard-colored tweeds, stoked to furnace heat on gin-and-lime, were wrangling about the relief of Lucknow; several old dragons in Edwardian hats and whalebone ruching sat frozenly crumbling their cheddar and the reputations of the younger matrons; and the painful foursome generally alluded to as Those Tahsome Ameddicans dawdled interminably over portions of plum-and-custard tart. It was futile to bullyrag the British guests, the headwaiter knew; they would linger on until their bones calcified or a heaven-sent stroke terminated the military maneuvers. But the outlanders were legitimate prey— indeed, in his varied experience, the Yankee tripper improved like the cantaloupe for being chilled and never seemed altogether content unless a light pressure of the spur was applied to his haunches. Investing his features with a ghastly apology for a smile, he ebbed toward the corner where my family and I, cloaking our shudders, toyed with the dessert.

"Anything wrong, sir?" he inquired, evincing the same bonhomie the captain at Voisin's might extend to a party of Okies. "I thought from your expression that an earwig might have fallen into the tart."

"No, no," I said hastily. "I stupidly left my artificial palate up in the room and I can't seem to pin down the flavor."

"Really?" he drawled. "We're rather keen on our pastry chef. He's been with us ever since Lord Febrifuge died."

"Well, I didn't attend the inquest," observed my wife, "but in our country, we use this sort of thing to poison crows."

"Rooks, madam," he corrected, compressing his lips.

"I can't seem to pin down the flavor," I said hesitantly.

"By the bye, did you know we were serving coffee in the Cenotaph Room?"

"Yes," she smiled. "That's why we're hiding in here." Our digestive juices stimulated to a free flow by the interchange, we arose and filed into the lounge. While hardly as delirious as Rampart Street during Mardi Gras, the scene that greeted the eye possessed a certain animation and sparkle. The fifteen or twenty manikins propped up in the cretonne armchairs occasionally cracked a knuckle or rustled the obituary page of the London *Times*, and now and again one of the more exuberant in the company so far forgot himself as to let fall some salty phrase like "extraordinary" or "simply smashing." As usually transpired whenever we appeared in public without our war bonnets and tomahawks, a look of utter incredulity spread over the assemblage. The entrance of a young Cherokee squaw in slacks, accompanied by two papooses in blue jeans and a brave whose sports shirt was undone at the throat, occasioned a gasp as marked as if Ann Corio had pranced in and begun executing a grind.

"Why are all those creeps staring at you?" my son asked his mother innocently. "Haven't they ever seen a lady in pants before?"

"It's because Mummy isn't wearing a girdle," his sister reported. For some curious reason, this artless deduction played ducks and drakes with the good woman's poise. She flushed the hue of a side order of Harvard beets, took a firm purchase on such juvenile skin as offered, and disappeared through the French doors into the billowing fog. I knocked a vase of lobelias off a table to render myself inconspicuous and sat down in the lee of a quintet of people discussing the Labour government. Three of them were elderly, horsy gentlewomen with bridgework that levitated forward in the manner of a railway cannon, their male escorts were, respectively, a gnarled old lion impersonating C. Aubrey Smith and a plump, aging refugee from a dovecot with cloth-topped high button shoes. The tenor of their remarks eluded me at first, but within ten seconds I was orientated. They were dissecting Sir Stafford Cripps and throwing him up for grabs with all the savage *élan* of Republican committeemen exhuming the peccadilloes of F.D.R.

"Traitor to his class," rumbled the craggy character, smoothing his meerschaum-tinted Guards mustache and swinging into the fine old familiar idiom. "Can't change human nature. Country's going to the demnition bowwows. Got to have brains at the top. Man's absolutely starkers—sheer, raving mad."

"That's what I'm told, too," said one of the ladies excitedly. "Clarissa Vavasour got it from her bootmaker's father-in-law that this stomach ailment he's supposedly treating in Switzerland——"

"Stomach ailment! Pah!" hooted the exquisite in the button shoes. "The fella's crackers! We all know he's up there at Davos with his vest buttoned backwards."

"Personally, I think he's only a tool," declared another of the dental trio. "The ones I'm fed with are Attlee and Bevin. I've heard they guzzle rare French wines right out in full view of the House of Commons."

"Ought to be horsewhipped, by gad," snapped the

old lion. "Hang 'em from the yardarm. Blow 'em out of the cannon's mouth, the way we did the Sepoys in '57." As they all fizzed off like Catherine wheels into denunciations of free wigs for the bald-headed and similar Socialist muck that had brought England to her knees, I decided it was plethora time and went out in search of Madame and the goslings. Under optimum conditions, Sidmouth might have seemed a reasonably appealing hamlet; the small brick villas nestling among roses and hawthorn had an elusive seedy charm, but eleven days of rain and mist had not intensified the allure. A sprinkle of mournful vacationists, bundled in waterproofs, shivered along the waterfront promenade and gaped incuriously at the gulls circling over the deserted pebbly beach. In a teashop wedged between a bankrupt fruiterer's and an establishment that repaired chipped Toby jugs, I ultimately ran down my quarry. The children were doggedly masticating slabs of a spongecake whose texture only Johns-Manville could have reproduced and my wife was composing a rough draft of a telegram to the Traveller's Aid Society.

"I can love, honor, and obey as well as the next man," she announced tremblingly, "but I've had all the gentility I can stomach. Either you spring us from that leprosarium or I'm taking the kids home on a cattleboat." Her rodomontade was superfluous, for I too was convinced by now that any further dalliance on Sidmouth's glacial strand was needless self-torture, a case of masochism in the cold, cold ground. At nine the following morning, we stowed our gear into the little

Moon-Glow tourer and raced northward through Here-
fordshire and Shropshire. It is, of course, breath-taking
rural country, and there is no more delightful way of
seeing it than from a well-sprung easy-chair in one's
own den, a tantalus of bourbon at the elbow and the
copy of *The National Geographic* partly tilted so as to
induce a comfortable drowsiness. Almost no tar gets
splattered onto the clothes (unless somebody happens
to be laying a road through the den), the danger of
windburn is cut to a minimum, and the second one
sickens of half-timbered taverns and Clydesdale horses,
he need merely lower his eyelids. The last, regrettably,
is a luxury denied the driver of a motorcar, and I consequently saw enough churchyards, hay-wains, and be-
smocked rustics to do me for some time. Our goal was
Liverpool, from which we had spontaneously decided
to fly to Dublin for a quick hinge; and before you
could say Kathleen ni Houlihan, we were planting our
standard in the lobby of the Shelbourne Hotel and proclaiming all steaks within a five-mile radius as our right-
ful fief.

It would be presumptuous, if not downright un-
healthy, to draw any generalities about Dublin from a
week's stay, but I found it a treasure, a city which immediately put me at my ease and gave me a sense of
self-identification. There was nothing starchy about it,
none of the withdrawn and marmoreal emphasis on
good form which embalms even trivial relationships in
England. Its people were lively, outgoing, independent,
and rarely smarmy; far from truckling to the visitor, in

fact, salespeople, cab-drivers, and waiters cultivated a salubrious attitude—known in Gaelic as the Strictly Drop Dead approach—that was extremely refreshing. The maxim seemed to be "If you don't see what you want, don't ask for it," and there was no hint of the constipating servility we had witnessed in the month past. Doubtless this was a reflection of Eire's recent political freedom, as well as of the profusion of goods on sale everywhere; the shops along Grafton and O'Connell Streets bulged with bacon, butter, coffee, cakes, confectionery, and clothing, and the clang of the cash register, as British sightseers snapped up the dainties unobtainable at home, furnished a cherry obbligato to the bustle of the town. The goose hung high.

After stuffing ourselves senseless at Jury's, the Central Hotel, the Dolphin, and a couple of other tip-top depots dispensing first aid to the needy carnivore, we opened our pores to Dublin's cultural pursuits with equal gusto. The Abbey Players proved to be even more enjoyable in their native habitat; theatergoing in a playhouse as attractive as theirs, filled with an audience responsive to skilled and witty actors, becomes the treat you remember from childhood. I did a fair amount of poking about the bookshops along the Liffey, not altogether successfully, as the sole item of interest I turned up was a soiled Gutenberg Bible reduced to three bob. I might have been tempted by it except that our bags were full of hand-woven linen and I feared the overweight on the return flight to Britain. We went also to a couple of small sociables attended by minor local literati and painters, where I had the stimulating experience of being taken aside by each of the guests and warned that his colleagues were expendable. "The man's a well-known polthroon and renegade," they hissed in turn. "He'd slit your gullet for a florin." Fraternal spirit in the arts had evidently changed little from the day of James Joyce—who, incidentally, I learned was currently the city's second largest industry, the first being the consumption of Guinness. Over ten thousand American university teachers are said to swarm into Dublin annually, all engaged in writing doctorates on some recondite aspect of *Ulysses* or *Finnegans Wake*. Busloads of the scholars were visible barreling about from Barney Kieran's snug to the martello tower, Phoenix Park, and other points mentioned in the sacred texts, and one enterprising curio dealer was even advertising such authentic bits of Joyceana as Molly Bloom's camisole and the very ashplant Stephen Dedalus had sported that epochal summer's morn.

It was a breathless mid-August evening three days later when I reined in the Moon-Glow at the door of the Mitre Hotel in Oxford. From Liverpool we had progressed arduously down into Derbyshire and the Midlands, a dreamy sequence studded with Spartan beds, largely inedible food, and the same wintry *politesse* accorded us at Sidmouth. The virtues of the British sports car do not include easy springing, and our collective bones throbbed with a Charley horse no colleen could know. What we required primarily was a double dose of the specific that knits up the ravell'd

"The man's a well-known polthroon and renegade,"
each one whispered in turn.

sleave of care; surely a night in Oxford's hushed clois-
ters would erase the ravages of the road and simonize
our tempers.

"Golly," yawned the mem, nuzzling her pillow. "It's
so wonderful and quiet. Let's never leave here."

"A deal," I said thickly. "I could sleep till the crack
of doom." As if in reply, the thunderous reverberation
of a thousand bells blasted the bedchamber, almost
splintering our eardrums. It had barely ceased before
another rolling salvo shook the windows. A hasty recon-
naissance disclosed a carillon recital stemming from the
tower of All Saints fourteen feet away. By the time it
finished, an hour and three quarters had elapsed and
our ganglia were pulverized to Rhode Island johnny-
cake meal. Toward midnight, as the triple bromides
were taking hold, din broke out afresh in the room overhead; a group of undergraduates, inflamed by Rupert
Brooke's verse and too many Lorna Doones, held a jam
session on washboard and kazoo featuring "Flat Foot
Floogie with the Floy Floy." The upshot was that
neither of us brought to our brief rubberneck tour next
day the dazzling clarity of mind or the erudition we
might have ordinarily. My wife kept referring to the
Sheldonian Theatre, where honorary degrees are conferred, as the Meltonian, which is more properly a shoe
cream, and I became so confused between Brasenose,
Balliol, Magdalen, and the Bodleian that I wound up in
a dim pub with a brush fire in the pit of my stomach
and my stays untied. The children fought a noble
rear-guard cultural action, however, by gouging the

shields of several colleges from the walls of their room, significant proof that they were emerging from puppy-hood into an awareness of things spiritual. On the whole, we had to admit upon quitting Oxford that the stopover had enriched all concerned, and nobody more lastingly than the management of the Mitre.

One of the more harebrained schemes born of a union of the Riviera moon and a bottle of Calvados had been our decision to cross the North Sea from England to Denmark, spend an *Augenblick* in the vicinity of Copen-hagen, and return to Paris via the Low Countries. In the frenzy of gestation, I took sweeping executive meas-ures, buying our passage outright and booking hotels with the prodigality of an Osage oil millionaire. The chickens now came home to roost; two nights later, Phileas Fogg and his three Passepartouts were aboard the *Prinsis Ingrid* en route from Harwich to Esbjerg, gobbling up herrings and akvavit and combing their Scandinavian phrasebooks for colloquial insults. A slight contretemps delayed us on arrival, when my interna-tional driving permit slipped down between the ship and the pier, but as soon as the water was pumped out of my lungs, we hummed away to Copenhagen in ex-cellent fettle. Darkness halted us at Odense, the birth-place of Hans Christian Andersen. The romancer's home, like most shrines of the sort, is rather unexciting. It is surrounded, though, by a cluster of souvenir shops whose mementoes surpass anything I have seen in the hemisphere for sheer vapidity. All the fanciful creatures conceived by the beloved storyteller have been re-created in appropriate materials like plaster of Paris, pipe cleaners, and burnt leather, executed with a lack of inspiration that leaves the onlooker speechless. The youngsters pestered me to hide them in one of the shops so they could watch the toys come to life at midnight, but I managed to stunt their growth just as effectively by narrating the histories of Landru and Lizzie Borden. Harassed parents would do well to avail themselves of the technique, for although it takes a bit of time and trouble, the resultant homemade nightmare is much superior to the crude manufactured product.

It may be that we were the victims of mass hypnosis in Copenhagen; perhaps it is not really a city of beautiful women, excellent restaurants, an amusement park harboring everything from a symphony orchestra to a roller coaster, and a generally civilized and leisurely way of life. If such is the case, my apologies to the Danish tourist bureau for thoughtlessly upsetting the saccharine bottle, but our interlude there was remarkably free of blemish. The hotel overlooked the Tivoli Gardens, in which are centered a score of cafés, open-air vaudevilles, a midway with all types of concessions, a concert auditorium, ballet theater, and every possible diversion including nightly fireworks. Our heirs and assigns instantly vanished into it, and for the first time in its one-hundred-and-four-year history, the ice-cream booths closed down for lack of stock. The scarcity of automobiles—Copenhagen still moves on two wheels— made walking a pleasure; sunk in an agreeable stupor, we drifted through the shopping district haggling over silver and porcelain we had no desire for, supervised the unloading of fish along the miles of wharves, contracted museum feet inspecting the Gauguins in the Glyptoteket, and, in a word, steeped ourselves in atmosphere and Carlsberg. The mood of the family became so maudlin in this halcyon environment that I finally was forced to rush them to a seaside resort on the Kattegat as an antidote. There, thanks to a ferociously bad hotel and worse vittles, we soon regained our normal perspective. The proprietor was a sullen countryman who divided his time between serving us dubious goulash made of Ken-L-Ration and dredging up aspersions about the United States. It was from him that I first heard American cars referred to as "dollar grins," a playful term engendered by their leering chrome grillework. Oskar was particularly winsome when he twitted us, as he did without surcease, with the superiority of Danish medical training to our own.

"I understand anybody can get a doctor's diploma over there, not?" he would venture with a malicious twinkle. "You go in the stationery store and buy one for a few pennies."

"You don't even have to do that," said my wife. "They enclose them in packages of breakfast food."

"And this qualifies a man to operate? Ugh, what barbarism!"

"Worse than that," I sighed. "You ought to see the butchers cut up their patients. Just like cold pork—no anesthetics, no sterilization, nothing."

"Horrible," he commented, licking his lips. "I must tell my friends in the singing society tonight."

"You will, Oskar, you will," rejoined the mem, stubbing out the cigar she had been puffing. "Well, abba dabba, I'm off to bed."

"Shall I turn on the hall light for you, lady?" inquired Oskar without shifting his hams.

"Don't bother, thanks," she said sweetly. "I'll just follow the roaches."

The pursy German official in the frontier control shack at Flensburg, gateway of the British occupation zone, thumbed through our passports to the visas granting us forty-eight hours to traverse the corridor, traced them with a cheese-paring nose as though they were printed in Braille, and beckoned us closer. It was shortly after dawn, and the long day's drive across Denmark topped by a crucifying sleepless night at Aabenraa told in our field-gray faces; we had the trig, zestful briskness of four bundles of wet wash.

"These are apparently in order," he said, disappointedly affixing his chop, "though you look much younger in the photographs."

"We've been through a good deal the past semester," I said morosely.

"So I see from your papers. Are you traveling for pleasure?"

"That was the way he sold it to me," replied my golden girl. "As your Mr. Schiller has aptly noted, the dream and the reality are frequently at variance."

"And how did you find conditions everywhere?"

"*Wunderbar*," I said. "Mankind's kicking the slats out

193

of his crib and car loadings are up all over. The millennium is right around the corner."

"Good, good," he beamed. Leaning closer, he lowered his voice confidentially. "Tell me, please, how does one go about getting to New York?"

"You took the words right out of my mouth, friend," I confessed, "but the moment I crack it, I'll drop you a postal." He sprang forward extending his hand impulsively, I sprang backward avoiding it, and hearts aglow with amity, we roared away into the Thousand-Year Reich.

He traced the passports as though they were printed in Braille.

12

The Roaring Traffic's Boom

PROFESSOR HENRI MANATÉE-DUGONG, staff clinician of the Hôpital Lariboisière, honorary member of the Royal College of Physicians and Surgeons, and the most eminent diagnostician in France, bounded from the limousine which had just whisked him across Paris in response to a midnight emergency call and scurried into the lift of the Hôtel Amérique du Nord. Donning the weary condescension of a plenipotentiary, the night concierge banged shut his ledger and approached at a snail's pace.

"Pull yourself together, idiot," rapped the doctor. "The American family who summoned me—where are they?" The retort surging to the concierge's lips died stillborn at the sight of the Legion of Honor rosette and the medical valise. He hastily slammed the door of the cage with a crash that dislodged thousands of flakes of bronze paint, and cables squealing, it swayed up the shaft. Before it was halfway to the sixth floor, I was speeding down the corridor to meet it, my face parchment-pale with anxiety.

"Bless you for coming, doctor," I said, fervently wringing his hand. "Believe me that I never would have called you if——"

"No excuses," Manatée-Dugong stopped me suavely. "A stranger in a foreign land—a crisis—I know how cruel it can be. Where is the patient?"

"In here," I motioned, "but first, am I correct in assuming that you are somewhat versed in tropical medicine?"

"To a small degree. I practiced nine years in Madagascar and French Equatorial Africa."

"Then our confidence is not misplaced," I said, relieved. "Allow me." As we entered the dimly lit bedroom, my wife looked up eagerly from the bed and her face brightened.

"Oh, doctor, we've been so frantic," she whispered, fighting back the sob in her throat. He patted her arm reassuringly, and drawing up a chair, extracted a thermometer from his vest.

"Ah—er—pardon me," I put in, "but there's nothing

wrong with Madame. I mean, there *is*, basically, but she's not the reason we sent for you."

"How stupid of me," he apologized. "It's one of the little ones, then?"

"Well, so to speak," Ibegan. "In terms of years——"

"Never mind the program notes," he interrupted. "Take me to the child."

"Well—uh—it's not strictly a child," I hedged. "It's more of a bird—our pet mynah, to be exact. You see," I said, talking swiftly because it seemed the best policy under the circumstances, "he was out in Siam—that is, I say 'he' though he might be a 'she,' who knows about birds?—anyway, we bought him out in Siam, but he's here now—right over in that corner——"

"One moment, please," panted Manatée-Dugong. A gobbet of foam, barely discernible against his graying goatee, flecked the edges of his mouth. "Do I understand, Monsieur, that you have had the crust to fetch the dean of the Faculté de Médicine of the Sorbonne here, at this supremely obscene hour, to attend a sick bird?"

"But he's not really *sick*, doctor," I pleaded desperately. "That's what I'm trying to tell you." The specialist peeled the toupee from his head for greater coolness and spread it on the floor while I divulged the pith of the story. In words that coruscated and glowed like precious stones, I described how we had driven at breakneck pace across Germany and the Lowlands in two days, seized with apprehension for the little feathered hostage we had left behind in Paris. I limned our

199

joyful reunion, told of the delicacies we had plied him with, the arpeggios and trills Tong Cha had poured out in thankfulness at his release. "And th-then it happened," my voice broke. "A couple of hours ago, when I offered him a scrap of veal remaining from dinner, he—he just put his head underneath his wing."

"Hm-m-m," muttered Manatée-Dugong, his scientific curiosity stirred despite himself. "This may be more complex than I thought." Rising, he paced up and down, absorbed in reverie. "Now try to remember," he said at last. "Has he eaten anything unusual today?"

"Nothing but a brioche, a box of zwieback, a plate of sauerkraut, two lady-fingers, an individual cream cheese, some goose-liver, and a napoleon. Oh, yes, and a bindle of lox."

"One more question." The diagnostician's frame suddenly stiffened and it was apparent he had already formulated a theory. "Has he ever accepted veal hitherto?" Aware how much depended on my answer, I asked guardedly what type of veal he meant. He picked up the toupee from the floor and distractedly tore it in half. "Veal, veal!" he shouted. "What the devil difference does it make?" My wife replied that it was the first the bird had ever seen. Manatée-Dugong slapped his thigh. "I was certain of it. A plain case of veal rejection."

"Is it serious, professor?" she implored. "These Oriental diseases——"

"Pouf! An avian whim," he shrugged. "He merely refused the morsel because it was unfamiliar and his crop

"Has he eaten anything unusual?" inquired the specialist.

was full." That anyone could so ably synthesize the facts and draw from them a brilliant conclusion reduced us to awed silence. As I numbly drew forth a wad of thousand-franc notes—which, with true Gallic disregard for money, he pocketed without counting—his austere professional manner relaxed, and he drew me aside. "Want to buy some real Parisian art photos?" he asked furtively. "No greengoods, John, every one a lulu." Not at all disconcerted by my rebuff, he threw down a peg of brandy, popped half a dozen packs of Stateside cigarettes into his satchel, and departed whistling. The whole affair, needless to say, had been a tremendously grueling emotional experience for us both, and it was small wonder that once the tension subsided, the dam broke and I gave way to floods of tears. My wife, sprung from a tougher stock that included generations of butchers and wheelwrights, was more stolid; she bathed my forehead with a sedative, forced eau de cologne between my teeth, and in a few minutes I was sunk in a dreamless sleep.

It would take the pen of an Émile Zola, combined with an electronic adding machine, to circumscribe our activities in the week that ensued, our last in Paris before embarking for home. Apparently some strange obsession seized my helpmate that our greenbacks were turning moldy, for there followed an orgy of spending that whipped up shopkeepers to a pitch of delirium and gutted the rue de la Paix. Rivers of perfume, sables, jewelry, lingerie, dresses, hats, gloves, and accessories poured into the hotel and poured right out again as I

returned everything to the stores. This tactic, it is superfluous to add, was not motivated by parsimony but an
earnest desire to keep the woman amused and stimulated. I knew that the moment her normal feminine acquis-
itive instinct was gratified, she would promptly lose
interest in the actual wares themselves, and so it proved;
on a hundred subsequent occasions, she expressed relief and gratitude that I had curbed her folly in time.
Occupied as I was in marshaling our prodigious baggage, bickering with steamship officials, and tickling
the chambermaids, I could not devote much attention
to our young, but I saw to it that they were not cheated
of the Bal Tabarin, the Moulin Rouge, and such corre-
sponding locales as might implement their education.
To engross them in the daytime, I assigned various
small diversions, like washing the family laundry in the
Seine and purloining vegetables from Les Halles, pastimes that engendered manual dexterity and self-re-
liance. It was a period of ferment and restless exertion,
in which we all worked doggedly shoulder to shoulder
dissipating what little energy and moola obtained after
nine killing months of travel; and when the last bat-
tered suitcase was flung down on the deck of the *Bagatelle* by its grumbling blue-smocked porter and the
docks of Le Havre began to recede, I sacrificed a plump
steward to Zeus and made an eternal vow about globe-
trotting, invoking wild horses, which nothing but a
dropped hat will ever persuade me to breach.

By a most curious coincidence, the *Bagatelle* was the
very steamer on which my wife and I had made our

honeymoon voyage to Europe two decades earlier. It was indeed significant, as I pointed out to her, that whereas our matrimonial craft was still eminently seaworthy, the vessel plainly showed the dismal ravages of time. (I forget exactly what answer she made, but I do recall that she took her head in her hands and rocked expressively to and fro.) An ineradicable smell of boiled cauliflower haunted the corridors, the shower fixtures alternately played dead and spat forth jets of steam that parboiled the bather, the lifejackets showed an alarming tendency to crumble in the hand. Without going so far as to suggest that she was an old firetrap, there was about the *Bagatelle* an air of combustibility that did not induce heart's-ease. Purely as a precaution, I slept the first night on top of the blanket with my shoes on, ears cocked for the siren calling us to abandon ship. My prudence naturally exposed me to a certain amount of ill-natured raillery, but nevertheless I made the family keep an extinguisher cached in the folds of a table napkin the rest of the voyage, ready to cope with overheated shashliks, crêpes Suzette, or any equally unforeseen hazard.

Generally speaking, a transatlantic liner America-bound at the end of summer has all the verve of a deserted amusement park. The exhilaration which buoyed up the tourist in Europe and powered his dizzy round of cathedrals, museums, and monuments has passed, leaving him the wan, cantankerous custodian of a bad travel hangover. He sits in the smoking room glumly contemplating a deflated purse and his imminent re-

All the verve of a deserted amusement park.

turn to the treadmill; with endless cognacs, he vainly seeks to appease a conscience racked with remorse at the fripperies he has purchased, the customs duties ahead, the responsibilities he has shirked. The passengers of the *Bagatelle* were no exception. Shuffleboard and deck tennis languished, the horse races folded for lack of patronage. All day long, our woebegone shipmates bent over writing-desks adding up columns of figures and sighing lugubriously. Fortunately, my wife and I were untouched by these megrims, inasmuch as we had on board a car which would permit us to drive straight from the pier, without any bothersome transition, to the nearest poorhouse. This automatically banished the specter of worry and left us free to grapple with a really vital problem, viz., the allocation of the gifts we were bringing back to our friends.

"Isn't that a beautiful negligee?" my wife exclaimed, emerging from a jumble of fabrics and fribbles amassed around the world. "Juanita'll be so thrilled that I bought it for her all the way out in Hong Kong."

"Well, you owe her a nice present," I said. "After all, she brought us that darling miniature bale of cotton the time she went to Memphis."

"It's a pity to waste such a lovely thing on her, in a way," she went on dreamily. "She's devoted to that sleazy old kimono she flaps around in."

"Why don't you keep it yourself?" I suggested. "It's uncanny how well it fits."

"I just noticed that myself," she said, startled. "I'll give her a pair of chopsticks instead. She hasn't any

"It's a pity to waste this negligee on her,"
observed my helpmate.

taste, and between you and me, I think she's treacherous. . . . Who gets those ruby cuff-links?"

"I earmarked them for Hirschfeld, sort of."

"No, they'll clash frightfully with his beard. You ought to wear them—they match your eyes perfectly."

"Good, then he can have this," I said, holding up a watch-fob. "He's always wanted a fob made of real human hair." If our intimates could have beheld with what zeal we selected their gifts, selecting for each the one most suited to his needs, they would have been inarticulate with emotion. The majority, as it ultimately transpired, were so overcome that they could not find words to acknowledge their feelings, but the words they did heated our home for months to come.

Two hundred miles east of the Dogger Bank, a devastating equinoctial storm struck the *Bagatelle* broadside on and almost wrote finis to the gallant old hulk. That I was instrumental in bringing her safely into port may sound conceited, but the facts are a matter of record. Immediately the crisis arose, the skipper sent me a note from the bridge. He had heard accounts over the nautical grapevine of how I had piloted the *Sembilan* through the tempestuous Banda Sea, and he beseeched me to retire at once to my bunk and stay there. The least disposition on my part to offer advice, he indicated, might have momentous consequences. Realizing that although it entailed personal self-sacrifice, all our lives were at stake, I acquiesced and sealed myself in the stateroom. Within thirty-six hours, the wind slackened, the ship had neared Ambrose Channel, and I was being lionized and feted out of all proportion to my trifling exploit. The newsmen who swarmed aboard at Quarantine threw out fulsome prophecies about Congressional medals of honor and the like, but I smilingly dismissed the affair with a jest. Just the same, it was with a consciousness of work well done that I strode the hurricane deck, watching the topless towers of Manhattan take form in the haze. Inconsiderable mite albeit I was, I had cut Father Neptune down to size.

About nine o'clock that evening, the two sunken-eyed customs inspectors who had been wrestling since midafternoon with our baggage collapsed on a carton of Royal Copenhagen porcelain and sponged their faces. Except for the cone of light flickering over the mountain of trunks, crates, barrels, hampers, and parcels before them, the great cavernous shed was in pitch blackness. By now all the *Bagatelle's* passengers were snugly ensconced in their hotels and apartments, restored by Martinis and busily boring relatives with adventure yarns; my own brood, sorrowfully protesting, had abandoned me hours before to attend a homecoming dinner complete with turkey and fixin's.

"Holy Moses," complained one of the inspectors wearily. "Tortoise shells, scimitars, brocades, automobiles—did you leave *anything* behind in those countries?"

"Only frogskins," I replied, uncoiling myself from a prenatal position atop a heap of duffel bags. "Listen, fellas, what about it? Why can't you take this stuff and let me go?"

"Not a chance," growled the other. "The government's got enough gurry as it is."

"Couldn't we push it off the end of the pier?" I begged. "Aw, come on, who's to know?"

"Uh-uh, thousand-dollar fine for blocking harbors and estuaries," he said. "Sorry, Mac, you'll have to pay off."

"But I don't want it!" I screamed, my voice echoing loonlike through the shadows. "I never wanted to go to Siam in the first place! You ask my wife—she's the one! She held a gun to my head, blackmailed me——"

"Yes, yes," said the first inspector soothingly. "Now blow your nose and let's get on with it. Where's this next item—seventy-two assorted sarongs, bamboo fans, and musical gourds?"

Some three weeks later, a golden Indian summer afternoon was fading into velvet twilight as I piled a final armful of excelsior and teakwood shavings into the dumbwaiter, nervelessly punched the bell, and plodded back into our living room. Though every muscle in my body ached from spurring on my wife, I had to confess she had done a creditable job of redecorating the nest and effacing the damage done by subtenants in our absence. Through long nights she had labored valiantly planing floors charred by cigarette butts; single-handedly she had kalsomined ceilings spattered by geysers of beer and repainted walls on which sportive hands had scrawled erotic verse in lipstick. But the scene that greeted my eyes repaid me for the patience I had lavished on her. It was a warm, friendly room, such a haven as those who travel far dream of returning to one day to treasure their memories. A shrunken head from New Guinea, its little cheek by jowl with a Javanese demon mask, grinned hospitably from the mantelpiece; a nine-hundred-pound Cambodian statue of the Buddha, writhing with cobras, dominated a corner; Balinese drums, Gujerati ikons, cowrie-shell boxes from Amboina, and basketwork from South Celebes were strewn around in planned confusion. Suspended on one entire wall was an illuminated showcase of old Hindu letters of credit and protested checks, and even the rug underfoot had been pressed into service to house the children's collection of geological specimens and stamps.

"Home at last," sighed my wife from the depths of her armchair. "To think that we covered twenty-five thousand miles."

"You made it seem like fifty, puss," I said with affectionate ambiguity. She started some footling retort, but the peal of the doorbell blotted it out. "Who on earth can that be?"

"Oh, probably some silly old process server or other," she yawned. "They start dipping in here like swallows toward evening." To my surprise, the caller was our building superintendent, a Mr. Thomas Carlyle (and oddly enough, a lineal descendant of the author of *Sartor Resartus*).

"Just dropped up to look your place over," he smiled. He gazed about admiringly. "Say, you folks sure been to a lot of places. Where you plan on going next?"

"Nowhere," returned my wife. "Me, I'm staying in this chair till the cows come home."

"Well, make with the pails, missus," he said, handing me an envelope. "I hear the bells in the pasture."

"Wh-what's this?" I quavered, recoiling.

"Your eviction notice," said Mr. Carlyle. "Building's coming down the end of the month. G'night, friends." As the door slammed, the heavy impact of a sun-bronzed body striking a divan sounded in the stillness, and a small balloon, containing the Siamese word for "zowie," ascended in the air. My wife picked up her highball and took a long, meditative pull.

"Have you seen my wool anywhere, dear?" she asked. "I think I'd better start knitting a new sweater for our passport. They say it gets terribly cold in Van Diemen's Land."

*It was a warm,
friendly room,
writhing with cobras.*